In the Name of the Father, and of the Son, and of the Holy Ghost. Amen.

THE SIGN OF THE CROSS

In the Nineteenth Century

BY

MONSIGNOR JEAN-JOSEPH GAUME
Protonotary Apostolic.

IN HOC SIGNO VINCES

By this Sign thou shalt conquer [Eusebius, *Vita Constantius.*, I, 22]

With a Brief from His Holiness, Pope Pius IX.,
(who attaches to the Sign of the Cross an indulgence of fifty days.)

TRANSLATED FROM THE FRENCH EDITION,
BY A DAUGHTER OF ST. JOSEPH.

𝕴𝖒𝖕𝖗𝖎𝖒𝖆𝖙𝖚𝖗.

ARCHBISHOP JAMES F. B. WOOD

Philadelphien:
Die 25, April, 1873

(*The Sign of the Cross in the Nineteenth Century,*
slightly arranged and retypeset from the 1873 edition.)

Originally printed by Peter F. Cunningham & Son
Catholic Booksellers, 1873.
Republished March 2017 © AMDG
ISBN 978-1544149769

Cover image: © User: Weglinde Gordon Lawson/Wikimedia Commons/
Public Domain (File: Central Panel All Saints Hove reredos.JPG)

Printed in the United States of America

DEDICATION

The Glorious St. Joseph.

O BLESSED FATHER ST. JOSEPH; Guardian of the Incarnate Word, Spouse of the Immaculate Mother of God, and Patron of the Universal Church, with sentiments of the deepest love and gratitude, I dedicate to thee this work, destined, I hope, to enkindle in many hearts, devotion to the Cross of Jesus, the shadow of which brooded so heavily, yet withal so gloriously, over thy life in Bethlehem, Egypt, and Nazareth.

Deign, O Holy Patron, to accept and bless it, that through thy intercession it may become to many the channel of the graces promised herein.

By the memory of the agony thou didst undergo during the three days' loss, I beseech thee, to take pity on those myriads of souls who have willfully lost their God, have separated themselves from Him and His Church, and rush blindly to destruction, ignorant or unmindful of their loss.

Thou art, according to St. Teresa, the Minister Plenipotentiary, the Treasurer General of the Most High. Open, then, those heavenly treasures; shed them on the children of the Church committed to thy care, and grant that by means of the Sign of the Cross, we may pass through life untainted by the vice and infidelity of the world. Let us not "glory, save in the Cross of Our Lord Jesus Christ," the instrument of our Redemption, the pledge of our eternal salvation.

THE TRANSLATOR .

Feast of the Presentation of Our Lady, Nov. 21st, 1872

PREFACE TO THE SECOND EDITION.

ONE word on the publication of this little work, and the unexpected success it has obtained. How did the idea of this book occur to us? Who arranged the unforeseen circumstances to which it owes its origin? Why does a work, destined to reawaken the faith of the Catholic world in the Sign of the Cross, appear at this time, and not two or three centuries ago? Why is it, that until now, no Pope thought of attaching a spiritual favor to that formula, the most venerable, most ancient, and most customary of our religion? How is it, that amidst so many solicitudes, Pius IX. has deigned to listen to our feeble voice, and hastened to admonish the Christians of our day to have recourse as frequently as possible to the Sign of the Cross, conformably to the example of their primitive ancestors? Why, in order to encourage them, has he enriched its use with an indulgence doubly precious? To all these questions we knew not, at first, what to reply. But now the light is made.

All comes to the point in the Church, for Divine Providence never gropes in the dark. Accustomed as it is, to use *that which is not, to confound that which is*, it shows itself no less admirable in small things than in great. The Sign of the Cross is, then, the arm of power against the demon. Instructed by the Apostles themselves, the early Christians knew it. In continual warfare with satan in all the power of his reign, and the cruelty of his rage; the regulator of morals, ideas, arts, theatres, festivals, and laws; the master of altars and thrones, sullying all, and making of all an instrument of corruption, they had incessant recourse to this infallible means of dispelling the fascinating charm, and warding off the fiery darts of the enemy. Hence, the continual

Sign of the Cross became for them an exorcism of every moment.

If, then, there appears now, without any premeditated design on the part of the author, a work designed to make the Christians of our day retake the victorious weapon of their ancestors; if, now withstanding so many adverse circumstances, this work spreads so rapidly; if it wins, even in Rome itself, the most august and precious of all suffrages; if, in fine, after eighteen centuries, the Vicar of Jesus Christ, the Chief of the eternal combat, by a solemn act, urges the Catholic world to have recourse incessantly to this sign, so victorious over paganism:—is it not reasonable to conclude that we find ourselves, in many respects, in a position analogous to that of the primitive Christians?

If they were confronted with satan, the king and god of that age; if they lived in the midst of a world that was not Christian, that wished not to become such, that wished no one to be such, that persecuted those who continued to be such;—are not we confronted with satan, who, unchained on the earth, is inciting nations to rebel against Jesus Christ, and making them cry out incessantly: "We will not have Him reign any longer over us"? And amidst what do the Christians of our day live? Are they not surrounded by a world that is ceasing to be Christian; that does not wish to return to Christianity, that does not wish others to belong to it, that persecutes in every possible way those who persist in doing so?

Cunning, violence, calumny, injury, blasphemy, sarcasm, spoliation, exile, death itself,—are not all employed against the children, as they were against the fathers? Arts, theatres, books, feasts, laws, sciences,—are they not now, as formerly, employed as weapons against Christianity? Is it, then, astonishing that the Sentinel of Israel, the Sovereign Pontiff, has come, by an act unknown in his predecessors, to reawaken the faith of Christians, by this Sign, the protector of the Church and society? The analogy is so striking that Protestants themselves are amazed at it. In their view, as in ours, there is no salvation for the present world but in the Cross. In the beginning of October a Prussian journal, the *Gazette of the Cross*, published a long article entitled: *By this Sign thou shalt conquer: In hoc signo vinces*. "To-day," said the Protestant writer, "we are engaged in spiritual warfare with the same antichristianism which Constantine, of old, vanquished with the material sword. Doubtless we should again say: 'Thou shalt conquer by this Sign: *in hoc signo vinces*.' The hidden and cruel powers of darkness rise to assault that Crown, by the grace of God, the key of the arch of the social Christian order."

Must not then the evil and the remedy be equally incontestable, when we see those same Protestants who formerly repudiated the Sign of the Cross as an act of idolatry, proclaiming the necessity of having recourse to it in these days, as a weapon, indispensable to us, if we wish to conquer the hidden and cruel powers, whose triumph would be that of barbarism?

The appearance, in some manner providential, of *The Sign of the Cross in the Nineteenth Century*, alone explains the rapid success which it has obtained. The first French edition was sold in a few months. Three translations of it have been made into different European languages—one in Rome, one in Turin, and one in Germany. Catholic papers have vied with one another in recommending its perusal, and many letters have been sent to us, bearing the congratulations of the most respectable men of France and foreign countries: *Soli Deo honor et gloria,* to God alone be honor and glory!

All agree to show the fitness of our humble work, and to enhance the greatness of the pontifical grace which is the eternal result of it. Let us quote only a few lines, begging those who wrote them to receive the expression of our sincere gratitude.

The learned Neapolitan review, *Scienza e Fede,* concludes its long analysis by saying, "What profit," will our society, immersed in materialism, exclaim, "what profit can humanity draw from this new work of Mgr. Gaume? Will it give help to the poor laboring classes, whom the revolution has deprived of work? Will it enroll volunteers for Poland? Will it exterminate the brigandage which is desolating Italy?   .   .   . It will do more than all this. It will give the bread of faith to those in want of it. It will enroll the Christians of the nineteenth century under the standard of the Cross, in the furious war which they have to sustain against the infernal brigand; under this Divine Standard, which has saved the world, and which alone can again preserve it   .   .   . Whatever the future may be, it will teach them how to be noble victors or noble victims; *in hoc vince.*"

Overjoyed at seeing an indulgence attached to the Sign of the Cross, the venerable Dean of the Catholic Chair writes: "An indulgence granted to the Sign of the Cross at your request!   .   .   .   .   . What will so many persons, whom I do not wish to name, say? The Holy Father has repaid with usury the pains you have taken in order to stop the paganism which invades us. By you and through you the whole Church receives the signal favor of an indulgence, extensive as the universe and durable as ages, which shall fall at every hour, at every second, as a refreshing dew upon the souls in Purgatory!

"How many blessings will those souls call down upon you! And if, at the time of your death, you be called on to pay them a short visit, what a reception will there await you!"

Let us pass to other testimonies, and come to those which have emanated from Rome. The Commission charged with the care of the regionary schools has thought it necessary to address the following circular to those who direct them.

"Among many books, useless and dangerous, particularly for youth, there are not wanting some that are useful, and well calculated to spread in the souls of youth the beautiful maxims of our august religion, and the love of its holy practices.

"One of those works is, unquestionably, that lately published by Tiberine, entitled *The Sign of the Cross in the Nineteenth Century*, which has been highly eulogized by many Catholic journals.

"The undersigned, while strongly recommending teachers not to permit in their schools any work not approved by the Commission, equally recommends them to cause the aforesaid work to be bought and read by their pupils. They may also use it as a premium at the annual Distributions which they are accustomed to have in their respective schools.

"Rome, from the Office of the Secretary of the Commission.
                                    L. PIERANO, *Deputy*."

LETTER OF HIS EMMINENCE,
CARDINAL ALTIERI,

PREFECT OF THE SACRED CONGREGRATION OF THE INDEX,

To Mgr. Gaume, Protonotary Apostolic.

Rome, August 7th, 1863

Most Illustrious Lord,

By the publication of your admirable work, *The Sign of the Cross*, you have rendered a new and signal service to the cause of the Church of Jesus Christ. In effect, you have made known to the faithful in the most attractive manner, all that is clearly contained, all that is taught, all that is operated in a most sublime manner of what is holy, divine, and consequently, sovereignly useful to souls in this sacred formula, as ancient as the Church herself.

The august Chief of this same Church, the Vicar of Christ, the Sovereign Pontiff, could not but receive most joyfully, a work so precious and useful to Christian people. Therefore, not only did he express his great satisfaction when I gave into his sacred hands the copy you hastened to offer him by my means, but he has, moreover, been pleased to grant, with kindness, the desire you expressed of seeing the practice of the Sign of the Cross enriched with an indulgence, thereby to incite them to make use of it for the defence of their souls, without any human respect, and as frequently as possible.

In the following Brief, you will see how bountiful the Holy Father has shown himself by the concession of such a grace, and how much it will cause its value to be appreciated. It is highly important that this new favor of the supreme dispenser of heavenly treasures, granted for the advantage of the Church militant, be universally known, at the same time that your excellent book shall be more widely spread and better appreciated.   In the Italian translation made of it by the incomparable Angel of Aquila, will be found the Brief, and it ought to be inserted in the new editions which certainly cannot fail to succeed each other.   In this manner shall be filled the void which you have signalized in the *Racolta delle Indulgenze.*

Thus, your Excellency shall receive the worthy recompense, and certainly, that most desired by your heart, in seeing the treasures of Redemption opened for the good of souls still living on earth, or already descended into purgatory, by the effects of the work you have composed with a view to draw the attention of every one to the first sign of the worship which all should render to the principal instrument of our Redemption.

Receive the expression of the sincere and high esteem with which

I am, Most illustrious Lord,
Your affectionate Servant,
L. Cardinal Altieri

Brief of His Holiness Pius IX., Pope.
For Eternal Remembrance.

Being fully certain that the salutary mystery of the redemption and the divine virtue are contained in the Sign of the Cross of Our Lord Jesus Christ, the faithful of the primitive Church made the most frequent use of this sign, as we learn from the most ancient and notable monuments. It was even by this sign that they began all their actions.

"At all our steps, all our motions, our incomings and outgoings, lighting the lamps, sitting down to table, taking a seat; whatever we do, or whithersoever we go, we mark our foreheads with the Sign of the Cross," says Tertullian.

Considering these things, we have judged proper to reawaken the piety of the faithful towards the salutary sign of our Redemption, by opening the heavenly treasures, in order that, imitating the beautiful example of the early Christians, they may not blush at making frequently, openly, and publicly the Sign of the Cross, which is the standard of the Christian militia.

Therefore, confiding in the mercy of Almighty God, and in the authority of His blessed Apostles, Peter and Paul, we grant, in the accustomed manner of the Church, to all and every one of the faithful of both sexes, every time that, at least, contrite in heart, and adding the invocation of the Blessed Trinity, they make the sign of the cross, fifty days indulgence for the penances which would have been imposed or that they should do for any reason whatever; we moreover grant mercifully in the Lord, that these indulgences may be applied, in the way of suffrage, to the souls who have departed this life in the grace of God. Notwithstanding all things to the contrary, these presents shall be in perpetuity.

It is also our will that the same credit be given to any written or printed copy of these presents, signed by a public notary, having the seal of an ecclesiastical dignitary, as would be given to these presents themselves, if they were shown or exhibited.

Also, that a copy of these letters be taken to the Office of the Secretary of the Sacred Congregation of Indulgences and Holy Relics, under pain of nullity, conformably to the decree of the said Congregation, dated January 19th, 1756, approved by our predecessor of holy memory, Pope Benedict XIV., the 28th of the same month and the same year.

Given at Rome, at St. Peter's, under the ring of the Fisherman, the 28th of July, 1863, the eighteenth of our Pontificate.

N. Cardinal Paracciani Clarelli

These present Apostolic letters, in the form of a Brief, dated July 28th, 1863, were presented at the Office of the Secretary of the Sacred Congregation of Indulgences on the 4th of August of the same year, conformably to the decree of the same Sacred Congregation, under date of the 14th of April, 1856.

In testimony of which, given in Rome at the same Office, the day and year as mentioned above.

Archbishop Prinnzivalli, Substit

CONTENTS.

First Letter

State of the Question — The Present World does not make the Sign of the Cross, or makes it seldom, or makes it badly — The Primitive Christians made it, they made it frequently, they made it well — We are right, and they were wrong, or we are wrong, and they were right; which is true? 19

Second Letter

Examination of the Question — Prepossessions in favor of the early Christians — First prepossession, their lights — Second, their sanctity — Third, the practice of true Christians in every age — Were the Fathers of the Church great geniuses? 24

Third Letter

Continuation of the third prepossession: The Doctors of the East and West — Constantine, Theodosius, Charlemagne, St. Louis, Bayard, Don John of Austria, Sobieski — Fourth prepossession, the conduct of the Church — Fifth prepossession, those who do not make the Sign of the Cross — Summary 30

Fourth Letter

Answer to one objection: the times are changed — Reasons in favor of the primitive Christians, drawn from the very nature of the Sign of the Cross — The Sign of the Cross is five things — A divine Sign which

Fifth Letter

Sixth Letter

Seventh Letter

Eighth Letter

Seventeenth Letter

Eighteenth Letter

Nineteenth Letter

Twentieth Letter

Twenty-first Letter

Twenty-second Letter

Twenty-third Letter

PREFACE TO THE FIRST EDITION.

IN the month of November of the year 1862, a young German Catholic—Frederic—of great distinction arrived in Paris to pursue his course in the College of France. Faithful, according to the traditional usage of his country, to make the Sign of the Cross before and after meals, he, on the first day, became the wonder of his school-companions. The next day, in virtue of the freedom of worship, he was the object of their mockeries. In one of his visits he begged us to tell him what we thought of the practice, of which his companions were trying to make him ashamed, and of the Sign of the Cross in general. The following letters are intended as an answer to those two questions.

THE SIGN OF THE CROSS

𝕴𝖓 𝖙𝖍𝖊 𝕹𝖎𝖓𝖊𝖙𝖊𝖊𝖓𝖙𝖍 𝕮𝖊𝖓𝖙𝖚𝖗𝖞

𝕱𝖎𝖗𝖘𝖙 𝕷𝖊𝖙𝖙𝖊𝖗

State of the Question—The Present World does not make the Sign of the Cross, or makes it seldom, or makes it badly—The Primitive Christians made it, they made it frequently, they made it well—We are right, and they were wrong, or we are wrong, and they were right; which is true?

Paris, November 25th, 1862

My Dear Frederic,

Scarcely fifteen days have elapsed since the newspapers announced the shipwreck of Captain Walker. This account, which we read together, was so much the more sorrowful, as by it we learned of the death of many of the passengers with whom we were acquainted. The vessel had struck upon a rock; the waves rushed in through the breach.

Notwithstanding the efforts of the sailors, it was impossible to close it. In less than an hour the hold was flooded. The ship visibly sank below the water-line. In the hope of saving it, they began to throw all the merchandise into the sea.

After the merchandise, the munitions of war, the furniture and part of the rigging. Then followed the provisions, excepting two or three casks of water, and a few bags of biscuits. All was useless. The vessel continued to sink, and its total wreck became imminent. As the last resource, Walker ordered the life-boats to be lowered; every one rushed into them. Unfortunately, the greater number, instead of safety, found there a watery grave.

With a few variations, this is, as you know, the history of every great shipwreck.

The unfortunate men, who, in such an extremity command the vessel, are perfectly excusable in casting into the sea everything that they can make away with. Life before everything.

The world of our day, that world which still calls itself Christian, and to which, no doubt, your young companions belong, presents more than one point of resemblance to a vessel damaged and about to perish. The furious tempests, which for a long time have incessantly beaten upon the vessel of the Church, have made large breaches in it, through which have entered many waves of antichristian doctrines, morals, customs and tendencies.

Woe, not to the vessel, which is imperishable, but to the passengers, who are not so!

What has it done? I speak not of the world openly pagan; its shipwreck is consummated. I speak of the world which still pretends to be Christian.

What has it done, what does it continue to do every day with the munitions of war and the provisions of life, with the merchandise, furniture and rigging with which the Church had supplied the vessel, that, notwithstanding the dangers of rocks and tempests, it might be assured of a successful voyage into the port of eternity? It has thrown them all, or nearly all, into the sea.

Where are the prayers that were formerly said in common in families? In the sea. Pious reading and meditation? In the sea. The blessing at meals? In the sea.

The habit of assisting daily at the Holy Sacrifice, the use of the scapular, and the beads? In the sea. The serious sanctification of the Sunday, by assisting at all the offices and instructions, by visiting the poor, the sick and the afflicted? In the sea. The regular reception of the holy sacraments, the obedience to the laws of fast and abstinence? In the sea.

The spirit of simplicity, of mortification, of modesty in dress, amusement, furniture, food and lodging? Where are the crucifix, holy images, holy water in apartments? In the sea, all in the sea. And the vessel still continues to sink. The Christian spirit is diminishing; the contrary spirit is increasing.

They cast themselves into skiffs, that is to say, into some kind of religion, which they make to suit their age, position, temperament and taste, and they live in this way.

Assisting at Low Mass on Sunday; and how? At High Mass, three or four times a year; at Vespers, never. Frequenting theatres and balls, reading everything that falls in their way, refusing themselves nothing but what they cannot get;—behold the frail skiffs to which they entrust their salvation! Can we be amazed at so many shipwrecks? Poor passengers, separated from the vessel, how much you are to be pitied! How much more to be pitied is the rising generation! Among the Catholic customs so imprudently abandoned by the present world, is one, precious among all others, which I would wish, at every hazard, to save from shipwreck. It is that which your companions despise, without being aware of it: I mean the Sign of the Cross. It is time to provide for its preservation. Yet a little while, and it shall have met the fate of so many other traditional practices, which we owe to the maternal solicitude of the Church, and to the intelligent piety of Christian ages.

Would you wish to know, dear Frederic, what is now the Sign of the Cross with those who pretend to be Christians? Place yourself on a Sunday at the door of a large church. Look at the crowd that enters the house of God.

A great number advance haughtily or foolishly, it is all the same, into the holy place, without even casting a glance at the holy water font, and without making the Sign of the Cross. As great a number pretend to take or receive holy water, and make the Sign of the Cross. You will see them dip their gloved hand into the holy water font, a thing as much against the liturgy, as to go to Confession or Holy Communion with gloves on.

As to their manner of making the Sign of the Cross, it would be better to say nothing about it; it is capable of puzzling the most learned explainer of hieroglyphics. A motion of the hand, careless, hurried, mechanical, and imperfect, to which it is impossible to assign a form, or give a signification, unless that the actors themselves do not attach the least importance to what they do;—behold their Sign of the Cross every Sunday.

Among that crowd of Christians you will scarcely meet any who make this venerable sign of salvation, carefully, correctly, and religiously.

If, then, in a public place and under such solemn circumstances, the greater number of persons do not make the Sign of the Cross, or make it badly, I can scarcely persuade myself that they make it, and make it well, in other cases, where there are, apparently, fewer motives to do so.

It is, then, an indisputable fact, that the Christians of our day do not make the Sign of the Cross, or make it but seldom, and very carelessly.

In this point, as in so many others, we are diametrically opposed to our ancestors, the Christians of the primitive Church. They made the Sign of the Cross, they made it well, they made it very often. In the East as well as in the West, in

Jerusalem, in Athens, and in Rome, the old and the young, the rich and the poor, priests and laymen, all classes of society, religiously observed this traditional custom. History affirms nothing more strongly. All the Fathers of the Church who were eye-witnesses, assert it, all historians prove it. Nothing would be easier than to cite their words. You will find them in the work *De Cruce,* by your learned countryman, Gretzer.

In the name of all, hear the words of Tertullian: "At every motion and every step, entering in or going out, when dressing, bathing, going to meals, lighting the lamps, sleeping* or sitting, whatever we do, or whithersoever we go, we mark our foreheads with the Sign of the Cross."

From this we are to understand, that at every moment our ancestors made the Sign of the Cross in one way or another, that they made it not only on the forehead, but also on the eyes, mouth, and breast.

Hence it follows, that if the first Christians were to reappear in our houses or publics places, and do to-day what they did eighteen centuries ago, we should be tempted to regard them as lunatics. So true it is, that in the use of the Sign of the Cross we are directly opposed to them. They were wrong, and we are right; or they were right, and we are wrong; either the one or the other; there is no medium. Which is true? Such is the question. It is grave, very grave; much more so than your companions, and those like them, think.

I hope to convince you of this in my succeeding letters.

Mgr. J.J. Gaume

---

* With hands crossed on the breast.

Second Letter

Examination of the Question—Prepossessions in favor of the early Christians—First prepossession, their lights—Second, their sanctity—Third, the practice of true Christians in every age—Were the Fathers of the Church great geniuses?

November 27th

My Dear Friend,

In ordinary cases, the exterior circumstances play an important part. They often have the value of direct testimonies in contributing to form the opinion of judges. You know that they thus examine the antecedents, position, and moral character of persons interested in the debate. Why should we pass them over in the case which occupies us? Therefore, before adducing the motives of the early Christians drawn from the very nature of the Sign of the Cross, let us examine together the prepossessions which militate in favor of their conduct.

First prepossession in favor of the early Christians:—They were contemporary with the apostles.

The Apostles had conversed with the Incarnate Word Himself, the Truth in person. They had seen Him with their eyes and touched Him with their hands. They were the depositaries and infallible organs of His doctrine. They had been commanded to teach it fully and entirely, nothing more, nothing less.

In their turn, the primitive Christians had seen and heard the Apostles, and their disciples. From their lips they had received the faith, from their hands, baptism. They had imbibed truth at its very fountain. With this truth, to which they owed everything, they nourished themselves; they made it the rule of all their actions, and preserved it with inviolable fidelity; *perseverantes in doctrina apostolorum* (persevering in the doctrine of the Apostles) [Acts II, 42]. Evidently, none have had better opportunities of knowing the thoughts of the apostles, and even of our Saviour Himself.

If then the primitive Christians made the Sign of the Cross at every instant, we are forced to conclude that they obeyed an apostolic recommendation; otherwise the apostles and their immediate successors, the infallible guardians of the triple deposit of faith, morals, and discipline, would have speedily interdicted a useless and superstitious custom, so well calculated to expose the neophytes to the mockery of the ignorant pagans. Therefore, I repeat it, in making so frequently the Sign of the Cross, the Christians of the primitive Church acted on very good reasons. This is the first prepossession in favor of their conduct.

Second prepossession in favor of the primitive Christians:—Their sanctity.

Not only were they well instructed in the doctrine of the apostles, but they were, moreover, most faithful to put it in practice. The proof of this is that they were very holy. Nothing is more clearly established, than that a high degree of sanctity was the general character of the early Christians.

First, they preferred to lose everything, their property and life itself in the midst of tortures, rather than offend God. Their heroism lasted as long as the persecutions, that is, for three centuries.

Secondly, they were very charitable. Heaven and earth have united in eulogizing their mutual love, unparalleled in the annals of the world. *Cor unum et anima una* (They had but one heart and one soul) [Acts, IV, 32], as God Himself said. Behold how they love one another, and how ready they are to die for one another! *Vide ut invicum se diligant et ut pro alterutro mori sint parati!* exclaimed the pagans.

Thirdly, they were filled with respectful love for the apostles, whom they obeyed with filial submission. St. Paul, who paid no compliments, writes to the Christians of Rome, that their faith is celebrated throughout the entire world; and to those of Asia, that they loved him so much, that had it been possible, they would have plucked out their eyes to give them to him. At his request, all the churches fly to the help of the brethren of Jerusalem, and Philemon receives Onesimus.

Fourthly, the Fathers of the Church, who were eye-witnesses, have continually rendered the most brilliant testimony to their sanctity. Addressing himself to the judges, praetors, and proconsuls of the Empire, Tertullian gave them this solemn challenge: "I appeal to your law processes, magistrates charged with the administration of justice. Among the multitudes of accused who are daily arraigned at the bar of your tribunals, is there a poisoner, an assassin, a profaner, a corrupter, or a thief, who is a Christian? It is your people who fill the prisons; it is yours that fill the mines; it is yours that fatten the beasts of the amphitheatre, it is yours who form your troops of gladiators. Among them there is not one Christian, unless he be there for the sole crime of Christianity." [Apol., c. 44.]

Fifthly, the pagan historians recognized their innocence, and their very persecutors rendered homage to their virtue. Tacitus, that author far too exacting and unjust with regard to our fathers, relates the frightful butchery of the Christians under Nero. *"Multitudo ingens,"* says he, "an immense multitude," perished amid the most frightful torments. They were innocent of that with which they were charged, but they were worthy of *odio generis humani* (the hatred of mankind)." Behold the word!

What, then, was this *mankind* of Tacitus? He himself tells us:—It was living filth, living cruelty. What caused its hatred? Because evil is the irreconcilable enemy of good, the sanctity of our fathers was the relentless condemnation of the monstrous crimes with which the pagans sullied themselves. Thence came Nero's butchers and his living torches.

Forty years after Nero, Pliny the Younger, governor of Bithynia, is charged by Trajan to inform against the Christians. Zealous courtier, he rigorously executes his master's orders, and causes our ancestors to be sought after. When put to the torture, he himself interrogates them. What is the result of his bloody proceedings? "All the crime of the Christians," writes he to Trajan, "consists in assembling together on a certain day before dawn, in order to sing the praises of Christ as of a God; in binding themselves by oath not to commit any crime, but to fly theft, robbery, adultery and perjury. I have caused them to be put to the torture, and have found them guilty of nothing but an evil and excessive superstition." [*Epist.*, lib. x, epist. 97.]

I have been expatiating, my dear Frederic, on the sanctity of our ancestors. In my mind, it forms the most powerful prepossession in favor of the Sign of the Cross. When men of this character, living in the face of death, show themselves invariably faithful to a usage, it must be that that usage is a little more important than your new companions believe.

Third prepossession in favor of the primitive Christians:—The practice of true Christians in the following centuries.

At a very early period there began to be formed, both in the East and the West, religious communities of men and of women. It is in those asylums, separated from the world, that we find the true spirit of the Gospel and the pure tradition of apostolic teachings, if not permanent, at least perpetuated with the greatest fidelity. The Sign of the Cross figures among the number of ancient customs preserved with jealous care.

"Our fathers, the ancient monks," writes one of their historians, "practiced the Sign of the Cross most frequently and religiously. They made it principally at rising, retiring to bed, before their work, in coming out of their cells and the monastery, or returning into it; they made it at table, over the bread, the wine and every dish." [Martène *De antiq. monach. ritib.*, Lib. i, c. i, n. 25, etc.]

In the world, in like manner, we find the traditional usage of this saving sign. All those great men, who, during more than five hundred years succeeded one another in the East and in the West; those incomparable geniuses whom we call the Fathers of the Church—Tertullian, Cyprian, Athanasius, Gregory, Basil, Augustine, Chrysostom, Jerome, Ambrose, and so many others who swell the list so terrible to pride, which it crushes by its weight; all those great intelligences practiced the Sign of the Cross most assiduously, and they incessantly recommended all Christians to make it on every occasion.

I have called the Fathers of the Church great geniuses and great men. If, as such, you compare them to your companions, expect a smile of pity; be not angry with them. Poor young men! They know the Fathers of the Church as they know their antipodes. In your turn, ask them what they understand by great men. In default of their reply, here is mine; it may be useful to you.

I call *great* men those, who, by the elevation, depth and extent of their genius, embrace the immense horizons of the world of truth; who know sciences, men, and things, not on the surface, but in their principles, end, and intimate nature; not only the matter below, but the spirit above; not only the man, but the angel; not only the creature, but the Creator; not only what is on this side of the grave, but what is beyond it, not one detail, but the whole; not one isolated law of creation, but the whole system, from which they cause to spring unexpectedly, luminous applications for the perfection of humanity. Behold genius, and behold the Fathers of the Church! You can challenge your companions to find among the ancients or moderns, any who have verified better, or as well, the definition of a great man.

However, renowned they may be in particular departments, in chemistry, physics, mechanics, or art, they are neither geniuses nor great geniuses. The man whose ideas embrace only one law, secondary to universal harmony, deserves not the name of *genius*; no one calls *great* the musician who can draw but one sound from his instrument, but only him who strikes harmoniously every chord.

Time does not permit me to finish my letter to-night; I will resume it to-morrow.

Mgr. J.J. Gaume

Third Letter

Continuation of the third prepossession: The Doctors of the East and West—Constantine, Theodosius, Charlemagne, St. Louis, Bayard, Don John of Austria, Sobieski—Fourth prepossession, the conduct of the Church—Fifth prepossession, those who do not make the Sign of the Cross—Summary

November 28th

My Dear Frederic,

Now, then, my dear friend, all those great geniuses, without any exception, made the Sign of the Cross like little children. They made it frequently, and unceasingly recommended Christians to make use of it on every occasion. "To make the Sign of the Cross," says one of them, "over those who place their hope in Jesus Christ, is the first and best known thing amongst us, *primum est et notissimum.*" [S. Basil. *De Sp. S.* c. xxvii.] Another: "The Cross is found everywhere; with princes and their subjects, with men and women, with slaves and freemen; and all mark it on the most noble part of the body, the forehead . . . Never cross the threshold of your houses without saying, *I renounce satan, and devote myself to Jesus Christ;* accompanying these words with the Sign of the Cross: *cum hoc verbo et crucem in fronte imprimas.*" [S. Chrys., Quod Christus sit Deus: et Homil. xxi, ad popul. Antioch.]

Another says: "We should make the Sign of the Cross at each action of the day, *Omne diei opus in signo facere Salvatoris.*" [S. Ambr., *Ser.* XLIII.] Others again: "Let the Sign of the Cross be continually made on the heart, on the mouth, on the forehead, at table, at the bath, in bed, coming in and going out, in joy and sadness, sitting, standing, speaking, walking; in short, in all our actions, *verbo dicam in omni negotio.* Let us make it on our breasts and all our members, that we may be entirely covered with this invincible armor of Christians; *armemur hac insuperabili christianorum armatura."* [S. Gaudent. episc. Brixien., *Trait de lect. Evang.;* S. Cyril. Hier., *Catech., iv.* n. 14; S. Ephrem. *de Panoplia.*]

Even to their last sigh, confirming their words by their example, we see those great geniuses die, like the illustrious Chrysostom, the king of eloquence, in making the Sign of the Cross. Formed in their school, the noblest Christians follow in their footsteps. Speaking of St. Paula, the grand-daughter of the Scipios, St. Jerome says: "When she was at the point of death, and we could with difficulty hear her speak, she placed her thumb on her mouth, and, faithful to usage, imprinted the Sign of the Cross on her lips." [Ad Eustoch. *De epitaph Paulæ.*]

Let us go back some centuries, and point out some brilliant links in the traditional chain. Without speaking of those immortal emperors, legislators, and warriors, Constantine, Theodosius and Charlemagne, so faithful to the use of the Sign of the Cross, let us come to the greatest of French kings, St. Louis. His friend and historian, the Sire de Joinville, has left us the following testimony: "At table, in the council, in the combat, and in every action, the king always began by the Sign of the Cross." [Vic. c. xv.]

Bayard, the knight "without fear and without reproach," is mortally wounded. Worthy of his life, his last act is the Sign of the Cross, which he makes with his sword.

Represented by two fleets of more than four hundred ships, the Catholic and Mussulman powers meet each other in the Gulf of Lepanto. On the combat depends the safety of civilization or the triumph of barbarism. The destinies of Europe are in the hands of Don John of Austria. Before giving the signal for attack, the Christian hero makes the Sign of the Cross. All the commanders repeat it, and Islamism suffers a defeat from which it never recovers.

Nevertheless, a century later, it tries to repair its defeat. Its innumerable hordes advance even to the walls of Vienna. Sobieski is called. Compared with those of the enemy, his forces are nothing. But Sobieski is a Christian. Before descending into the plain, he makes the Sign of the Cross on his army; he himself forms a living sign, by hearing Mass with his arms extended in the form of the Cross. *It was there*, says a Christian warrior, *that the Grand Vizier was overcome.*

I should never conclude, my dear friend, were I to cite, one after the other, all the facts which prove the perpetuity and frequent use of the Sign of the Cross among the true Christians of every age and condition, in the world as in the cloister; in the East as in the West. Does not this glorious tradition form a passably respectable proof in favor of our ancestors of the primitive Church? What do your young companions think of it?

Fourth prepossession in favor of the primitive Christians:—The usage of the Church.

Ages roll by, and with the times, men change. Laws, customs, fashions, language, manners of seeing and judging, all are modified. The Church alone changes not. Immutable as truth, of which she is the mistress, that which she taught, that which she did yesterday, she teaches, she does to-day; she will teach, she will do to-morrow and always.

What are her thoughts, what is her conduct with regard to the Sign of the Cross? There is no point on which her divine immutability is more clearly manifested. For eighteen centuries we may say the Church has lived on the Sign of the Cross. She has not, for a single instant, ceased to employ it. She commences, continues, finishes everything by this sign.

Among all her practices, the Sign of the Cross is the principal, the most ordinary, the most familiar. It is the soul of her exorcisms, prayers and benedictions.

What we see her do in our sight, in our basilicas, she did in that of our fathers in the Catacombs. "Without the Sign of the Cross," say they, "nothing is done validly, nothing is perfect, nothing is holy." [S. Cypr. *De bapt. chr.*—S. Aug., *Tract* 128, *in Joan., n.* 5.]

The power of the Church, like that of her divine Founder, is exercised on creatures, and on man. It extends to heaven and earth: *Data est mihi omnis potestas in cœlo et in terra* (All power is given to Me in Heaven and on Earth). [St. Matt. XXVIII, 18]

How does she exercise it? By the Sign of the Cross. All that she destines for her use—water, salt, bread, wine, fire, stone, wood, oil, balm, linen, silk, brazen figures, precious metals—all that belongs to her children; their dwellings, flocks, implements of labor, the inventions of their industry—she takes possession of all by the Sign of the Cross.

If she wishes to prepare an earthly dwelling for the God of heaven, first of all, the Sign of the Cross must consecrate the site of the edifice. "Let no one," say the Councils, "dare to build a Church without calling the Bishop to the place, that he may make the Sign of the Cross there, in order to chase away the demons." [Novella *V. paragraph* 1. *Cap. Nemo de Consecrat. dist.* 1.]

The Sign of the Cross is the first thing she employs to bless the materials of the temple. She traces it twenty times upon the pavement, on the pillars, on the altar. To render it permanent, she makes it of iron, and places it on the summit of the edifice. When her children come into the house of God, what do they do before crossing the threshold? They make the Sign of the Cross.

By what do the chiefs of prayer, the bishops and priests,

begin to celebrate the praises of the Most High? By the Sign of the Cross.

"When at the beginning of the Office we make the Sign of the Cross, saying the words, *O God, come to my aid,* it is as if we would say," writes an ancient liturgist, "Thy Cross, O Lord, is our help; the hand makes to Thee the Sign of it, and the tongue prays to Thee in it. The demon is the chief of the enemies of our salvation; he governs the world, he flatters the flesh in order to allure us. If then, O Lord, Thou wilt aid us by Thy Cross, he and all our enemies shall be put to flight." [Reasons for the Office, etc. p. 270.]

See principally the conduct of the Church towards man, the living temple of the Blessed Trinity. The first thing she makes over him after his birth is the Sign of the Cross; the last, when he returns to the bosom of the earth is again the Sign of the Cross. Behold her first greeting, and her last farewell to the child of her tender affection!

Within the time that intervenes between the cradle and the grave, how many times is the Sign of the Cross made on man?

At his baptism, in which he is made the child of God, the Sign of the Cross; at his Confirmation, in which he becomes the soldier of virtue, the Sign of the Cross; in the Holy Eucharist, in which he is fed with the bread of angels, the Sign of the Cross; in Extreme Unction, in which he is strengthened for the last combat, the Sign of the Cross; in Holy Orders and Matrimony, in which he is associated to the paternity of God Himself, the Sign of the Cross. Always and everywhere, now as in former times, in the East as in the West, the Sign of the Cross is made on man. [S. Chrys., *in Math. homil.* 54, n. 4. *S. Augus. in Joan. tract.,* 128, n. 5.]

All this is yet nothing. Behold what the Church does, when,

in the person of the priest, she ascends the altar. Armed with omnipotence which has been given her, she comes to command, no longer a creature, but the Creator; no longer a man, but God. At her voice, the heavens are opened; the Word again becomes incarnate, and renews all the mysteries of His life, death, and resurrection. Is there an act which ought to be performed with more solemn gravity? An act from which should be more carefully banished everything that might be foreign or superfluous?

Now, in the course of this, the *action*, by excellence, the Church, more than ever, multiplies the Sign of the Cross; she clothes herself with the Sign of the Cross; she goes through it with the Sign of the Cross; she repeats it so frequently, that the number of times would seem to be exaggerated, were it not so profoundly mysterious. Do you know how many times the priest makes the Sign of the Cross during Mass? He makes it *forty-eight times!* I am wrong; throughout the whole of the august sacrifice, the priest is himself a living Sign of the Cross.

And the Catholic Church, the grave teacher of nations, the great mistress of truth, does she amuse herself by repeating so frequently in her most solemn act, a sign, useless, superstitious, or of minor importance? If your companions believe this, they are wrong to call themselves unbelievers: it is not credulity that is wanting to them.

The conduct of the Church and of true Christians in every age, is, then, a victorious prepossession in favor of our primitive ancestors.

Fifth prepossession in favor of the early Christians:— *Those who do not make the Sign of the Cross.*

There are on earth six classes of beings that do not make the Sign of the Cross.

First, pagans: — the Chinese, Hindoos, Thibetans, Hottentots, and the savages of Oceanica, adorers of monstrous idols, nations most deeply degraded, yet not the less unhappy — they do not make the Sign of the Cross.

Second, the Mahometans: — swine by sensuality, tigers by cruelty, automata, by fatalism, — they do not make the Sign of the Cross.

Third, the Jews: — deeply encrusted with a thick layer of superstition, the living petrifaction of a fallen race — they do not make the Sign of the Cross.

Fourth, Heretics: — impertinent sectaries, who have pretended to reform the work of God, who, in punishment of their pride, have lost even the last remnant of truth. "I affirm," said one of your Prussian ministers lately, "that I could write on my thumb nail all that remains among Protestants of common belief:" — Protestants do not make the Sign of the Cross.

Fifth, bad Catholics: — renegades to their baptism, slaves of human respect, haughty in their ignorance, who speak of everything, yet know nothing; adorers of the god of their belly, of the god of the flesh, of the god of matter; whose private life is like a sullied garment — they do not make the Sign of the Cross.

Sixth, beasts, bipeds and quadrupeds of all kinds: — dogs, cats, asses, mules, camels, owls, crocodiles, oysters, hippopotamuses — they do not make the Sign of the Cross.

Such are the six classes of beings that do not make the Sign of the Cross.

If, before tribunals, the moral character of the plaintiffs or defendants contributes powerfully to form the opinions of the judges, even before the examination of the cause, I leave you to judge whether the character of the beings who do not make the Sign of the Cross is a small prepossession in favor of the early Christians.

In a word, with regard to the frequent use of the Sign of the Cross, the world is divided into two opposite parties.

For it:—The admirable Christians of the primitive Church; the holiest and greatest geniuses of the East and the West; the true Christians of every age; the Church herself, the Mistress of truth.

Against it:—Pagan, Mahometans, Jews, Heretics, bad Catholics, and beasts.

It seems to me that you can already decide; moreover, your convictions shall be more strongly confirmed, when you learn the motives which justify the one, and condemn the other. I will reveal them in the following letters.

Mgr. J.J. Gaume

Fourth Letter

November 29th

My Dear Frederic,

"As for me," I hear you say, my dear Frederic, "the question is decided. Never will I believe that God has given truth and good sense to His enemies, and at the same time condemned His best friends to error and superstition."

This avowal rejoices, yet does not surprise me. Your mind seeks the truth, and your heart does not reject it. If all were in the like dispositions, the apologist's task would be easy. Unfortunately, it is otherwise. In the greater part of controversies, particularly religious controversies, men argue not according to reason, but according to their passions. They combat, not for truth, but for victory. Sad victory, which more strongly confirms them in the slavery of error and vice!

What I know of your companions, and so many other pretended Catholics of our day, gives me reason to fear they are ambitious for this fatal victory alone. I love them too much not to contest it with them. In order to remove the bandage with which they cover their eyes, as well as to strengthen yet more your own convictions, I shall expose the intrinsic reasons which justify the inviolable fidelity of true Christians to the frequent use of the Sign of the Cross.

Let us first do justice to the great object of modern contemners of the adorable Sign. "Other times, other manners," say they. "What was useful, nay, even necessary in the first ages of the Church, is not so now. Times are changed;

we must live according to the manners of the day."

St. Paul answers them: *Jesus Christ yesterday, and to-day and the same forever.* [Hebrews XIII, 8]

Tertullian adds: *The Incarnate Word calls Himself Truth, and not Custom.* Truth, then changes not. What the apostles, the Christians of the primitive Church, and the true Christians of every age have held to be useful, and to a certain extent, even necessary, has not now ceased to be so. I dare even affirm it to be more necessary now than ever.

This is on account of the many points of resemblance which exist between the situation of the primitive Christians, and that of the Christians of the nineteenth century.

What was the situation of our forefathers of the primitive Church? They were in the midst of a world which was not Christian, which did not wish to become so, and which persecuted those who persisted in being so.

And are we not in the midst of a world that is losing Christianity, that does not wish to return to it, and that persecutes, sometimes by violence, those who persist in professing it?

If, in a like situation, the first Christians, formed in the school of the apostles, regarded as necessary the frequent use of the Sign of the Cross, why should we abandon it? Are we stronger or more skilful? Are our dangers less great, our enemies less numerous or perfidious? To propose such questions is to decide them. Let us proceed.

Until now, my dear Frederic, I have established only the exterior circumstances of the cause: it is necessary now to examine it in its depth, by adducing reasons drawn from the very nature of the Sign of the Cross.

For you, for me, for all sensible men, they may be summed

up as follows:—We are children of the dust, the Sign of the Cross is a divine Sign, which ennobles us; we are ignorant, it is a book which instructs us; poor, it is a treasure which enriches us; soldiers, it is a weapon which puts the enemy to flight; travelers on the way to heaven, it is a guide that conducts us.

Assume the insignia of a judge, ascend your tribunal, and hear the cause.

We are children of the dust; the Sign of the Cross is a divine Sign, which ennobles us.

Tell me who is that being that comes into the world weeping; who crawls like the worm, who, like the smallest animal is subject to every infirmity, and for even a longer time than it, is incapable of supplying his own wants?

Let the man who is called prince, king, or emperor; the woman who is called countess, duchess, or empress, be not too proud.

One glance backward will tell them who that being is: it is man, a worm of the earth in the cradle, the food of worms in the tomb. [Sap. vii., 34.—Plutarch, *Lib. de amore prolis.*]

That being so low, so useless, and during the first stages of his existence, so ignominiously confounded with the weakest and vilest of animals, is, moreover, but too much inclined by his instincts to resemble them. Nevertheless, that being is the image of God, the king of creation; he must not degrade himself. God touches him on the forehead, and imprints a Divine Sign which ennobles him. Nobility imposes obligations. Respected by others, he will respect himself. This patent of nobility, this divine mark, is the Sign of the Cross. It is divine, since it comes from heaven, since the owner alone has the right to stamp his property with his image. It comes from heaven, since earth avows that it did not invent it. Go through every country and every age, nowhere will you find the man that invented it, the saint that taught it, the council that imposed it. "Tradition teaches it," says Tertullian, "custom confirms it, faith practices it." [Tertullian, *De Coron. Mil.*, c. iii.]

In Tertullian you hear the latter part of the second century of the Church. St. Justin speaks for the first, and teaches not only the existence of the Sign of the Cross, but the manner in which it was made. [*Quæst.* 118.] Behold us in those primitive times, days of eternal memory, called even by heretics the "Golden Age" of Christianity, on account of the purity of its doctrine, and the sanctity of its morals. Here, then, we find the Sign of the Cross in full practice, in the East and the West.

Let us go back a few steps and we shall clasp hands with St. John, the last survivor of the apostles. See the venerable old man, making the Sign of the Cross over the poisoned cup, and drinking the deadly liquor with impunity. [S. Simeon, *Metaph. in Joan.*]

A few steps farther, and we meet his illustrious colleagues, Peter and Paul. Like John, the beloved disciple of the divine Master, Peter and Paul, the Princes of the Apostles, make religiously the Sign of the Cross, and teach it from the East to the West, in Jerusalem, Antioch, Athens, and Rome, to Greeks and barbarians. Let us listen to an unexceptionable witness of tradition. "Paul," says St. Augustine, "carries everywhere the royal standard of the Cross. He fishes for men, and Peter marks the nations with the Sign of the Cross." [*Serm.* xxviii.]

They make it not only over men, but also over inanimate creatures, and cause others to do the same. "Every creature of God is good," writes the great apostle, "and nothing to be rejected that is received with thanksgiving; for it is sanctified by the word of God and prayer." [I Tim. 4:4-5.]

Such is the rule. What is the sense? In the study of law, if we meet with an obscure passage, what do we do? To elucidate it, we consult the interpreter best authorized and nearest to the legislator; his word is law.

Listen to the best authorized interpreter of St. Paul, the great Chrysostom. "Paul," says he, "here establishes two things; the first, that no creature is unclean; the second, that supposing it to be so, the means of cleansing it is at hand. Make the Sign of the Cross over it, render thanks and glory to God, and at the same instant, all uncleanness shall disappear." [In Tim., *Homil.* xii.] Behold apostolic teaching!

The princes of the apostles made the Sign of the Cross not only over inanimate creatures, and the multitudes who received the faith from them, but on themselves also. This sign, then, existed before them. Paul the persecutor, is thrown down on the road to Damascus. He must become the apostle of the God whom he pursues. What will be the first act of that victorious God? To mark the vanquished with the Sign of the Cross. "Go," says He to Ananias, "go, and mark him with my sign." [S. Aug. *serm. I. et* xxv. *de sanctis*]

Who then is the author and institutor of the Sign of the Cross? To find him we must go beyond all ages, all visible creatures, all angelic hierarchies; we must rise to the Eternal Word, the Truth in person.

Listen again to a witness who was so situated as to know it perfectly, a witness so irreproachable that he has sealed his testimony with his blood. I mean St. Cyprian, the immortal Bishop of Carthage. "O Lord, Holy Priest," exclaims he, "Thou hast bequeathed to us three imperishable things: the chalice of Thy Blood, the Sign of the Cross, and the example of Thy sufferings." [Ser. *de Pass. Chr.*]

St. Augustine adds: "It is Thou that hast willed this Sign should be imprinted on our foreheads." [*In ps.* 130]

It would be easy to cite twenty other witnesses, but as I am writing letters and not books, I will stop. The Sign of the Cross is a Divine Sign: this is the first fact established in the discussion. There is another, of which I shall speak tomorrow.

Mgr. J.J. Gaume

Fifth Letter

The Sign of the Cross ennobles us—It is the exclusive Sign of the elite of humanity—It is the escutcheon (coat-of-arms) of Catholicity—What a Catholic is—By ennobling us, the Sign of the Cross teaches us the respect due to ourselves—Importance of this lesson—Disgrace of those who do not make this sign—Picture of the contempt they have for themselves

November 30th

My Dear Frederic,

I have added, my dear Frederic, that the Sign of the Cross is a Sign which ennobles. It ennobles us because it is divine. All that is divine is ennobling. This reason alone might dispense with every other, nevertheless, I add that it ennobles us, because it is the exclusive Sign of the *élite* of humanity. Have your companions ever reflected on this?

All who do not make the Sign of the Cross, and much more, all who are so unfortunate as to blush at it, remain confounded with Pagans, Mahometans, Jews, Heretics, bad Catholics and beasts, that is to say, with the very dregs of creation. What do you think of this? Have we not reason to be proud of that which distinguishes us from those who do not bear it?

A child is proud of belonging to a family venerable for its antiquity, illustrious for its services, respected for its virtue, powerful, by its riches. Again, how jealous he is of his escutcheon! He carves it in stone, marble, silver, gold, agate or ruby; he engraves it on his dwelling, sculptures it on his furniture, enchases it on his plate, and marks it on his linen; he bears it on his seal, would wish to carry it on his forehead. It is painted on the panels of his carriage, and even the harness of his horses is decorated with it. Leaving vanity aside, he is right. His conduct proclaims the eminently social law of solidarity. The glory of their forefathers is the glory of the children; it is the family patrimony.

Being a Catholic, the Sign of the Cross is my escutcheon. It proclaims to me and to every one, the nobility of my race, its antiquity, its services, its glories and its virtues. And I not be proud of it! I should then deny the illustrious blood that courses through my veins! Unworthy to bear a great name, I should basely repudiate the law of solidarity, throw my coat-of-arms into the mire, and cast to the winds the rich inheritance of my ancestors.

Men are proud of belonging to an aristocratic nation. The Spaniard is proud of being Spanish; the Englishman, of being English; the Frenchman of being French, and so with other great nations.

Tell me, my friend, which is the grandest, the most aristocratic nation on the globe?

It is a nation more ancient, and which in itself alone, has a greater number of citizens than all those I have named; a nation, which by its light, shines in the world like the sun in the firmament; a nation essentially expansive, which, at the price of its blood, has drawn the human race out of barbarism, and, at the same price, prevents it from falling back into it again, as is proved by history and the map of the world; a nation among whose children alone are found all that man has known as great by genius, virtue, science and courage; whole legions of doctors, virgins, martyrs, orators, poets, philosophers and artists; the great legislators, good kings, and illustrious warriors in every part of the world; a nation so much the more aristocratic, that to her all others owe their superiority. No matter what may be said or done, history points this out as the great Catholic nation. I belong to it. The Sign of the Cross is its escutcheon, and shall I be ashamed of it?

God Himself has deigned to show by striking miracles, how honored in His sight are the person and the member that make the Sign of the Cross.

St. Edith, daughter of Edgar, King of England, from her very infancy, bore the Sign of the Cross in her heart. This little princess, one of the most beautiful flowers of virginity that have adorned the former Isle of Saints, did nothing without first making this salutary sign on her forehead and breast.

Having caused a church to be built in honor of St. Dionysius, she begged St. Dunstan, archbishop of Canterbury, to come to dedicate it. He did so willingly, and in several interviews which he had with the Saint, he was struck at seeing her make so frequently the Sign of the Cross on her forehead with the thumb, according to the custom of the early Christians.

This devotion pleased him so much that he begged God to bless that thumb, and even to preserve it from the corruption of the grave. His prayer was granted.

The Saint died soon after, at the age of twenty-three years, and, appearing to the holy bishop, said: "Raise my body from the tomb. You will find it incorrupt, with the exception of those members, of which, in the levity of my childhood, I made a bad use."

Those members were her eyes, feet and hands, which, in effect, were found to be decayed, except *the thumb*, with which she had so often made the Sign of the Cross. [See her Life, viii.]

As regards the point of honor, were our ancestors wrong in making such frequent use of the Sign of the Cross? Are we right in not making it?

Alas! Far different from ours was the pride of their nobility, the feeling of their dignity! By dwelling so much on the obligations of that dignity, I do not wonder at their having established a society, which, for the heroism of its virtues, is without parallel in the annals of the world: you will now begin to understand it.

The first sentiment that the Sign of the Cross inspires us with, is respect for ourselves, because it ennobles us. Respect for ourselves! Dear friend, what a great thing I have said. I look around me; I see an age, a world, a rising generation which talks incessantly of the dignity of man, of emancipation, of liberty. These words, either void of meaning, or filled with an evil one, render the age, the world, the generation, ungovernable. Impatient of the yoke of all authority, divine, social, civil, or parental, they continually cry out to all they meet: "Respect me!"

Very good; but if you wish to be respected, begin by respecting yourself. The respect of others for us is proportioned to that which we have for ourselves. Cruelty, hypocrisy, debauchery, vice gilded, gloved, painted, plumed, spurred and crowned, may inspire fear, but can never win respect. Now, then, the man of the day, whether he be old or young, who does not make the Sign of the Cross, does he respect himself? Let us make a trial by autopsy.

The noblest part of man is the soul; the noblest faculty of his soul is the intelligence. Precious vessel, formed by the hand of God Himself to receive truth, and nothing but the truth! All that is not truth defiles and profanes it. Does the man of our day respect it? Is it truth that he deposits therein? He has nothing but disgust for its pure sources whence it flows. Divine oracles, sermons, books of asceticism, or Christian philosophy, fill him with loathing.

If you descend into that baptized intelligence, you will think yourself to be in a storehouse of odds and ends. There you find jumbled together, pell-mell, ignorance, idle tales, frivolity, prejudices, lies, errors, doubts, objections, denial, impieties, silliness and trifles. A sad spectacle, which reminds me of an ostrich that died lately in Lyons. You know that in the autopsy, one of the stomachs of the stupid animal was found to be a regular storehouse of old iron, ends of ropes, and pieces of wood.

Such is the intellectual nourishment of the man who does not make the Sign of the Cross. Behold how he respects it!

And his heart? Excuse me, my dear Frederic, from revealing to you its ignominy. Its emotions, instead of being directed upward, tend downward. Instead of soaring like the eagle, it crawls like the worm; instead of feeding like the bee on the perfumed juice of flowers, like the stercorary fly it rests only on filth. There is no violation of the immaculate law from which it recoils, no pollution which it avoids; and, as you know that from the abundance of the heart the mouth speaks, the throat is, like the vent-hole of a sepulchre, full of corruption. [Sepulcrum patens est guttur eorum (Their throat is an open sepulchre.) Ps. v. 11.]

And his body? Young man, who think it beneath you to make the Sign of the Cross, you believe yourself very clever; you are to be pitied. You think yourself independent; you are a slave. You refuse to honor yourself by doing what the *élite* of mankind do; by a just judgment, you shall dishonor yourself by the most shameful acts of the dregs of humanity.

Your hand will not trace the Divine Sign on your forehead, but it will touch what it should never touch.

You will not defend your eyes, lips, or breast with this

protecting Sign; your eyes shall be sullied by looking at what they should never see; your lips, talkative yet dumb, *loquaces multi*, as says a great genius, [S. Aug. Med. xxxv. 2.] shall say nothing that they should, and everything they should not; your breast, a profane altar, shall burn with a fire the very name of which is a disgrace. This is private history. You cannot deny it; you cannot efface it. Written here with ink, it may be read on every part of your being, written with the blood of sin, *in sanguine peccati.*

And his life? The man who does not make, or who has ceased to make the Sign of the Cross, loses all esteem of his life. He despises it, he squanders it, for he never takes it in earnest. To turn night into day, and day into night; to work little, sleep much, fare sumptuously; to refuse nothing to his appetites; to spend time without any regard to eternity, that is to say, in weaving cobwebs, catching flies, and building card-castles; in a word, using his life as if he were the proprietor of it: this is not taking life in earnest. To take life in earnest, is to use it according to the will of Him who gave it to us, and who will demand a rigorous account of it, not as a whole, but in detail; not by the year, but by the moment.

When the despiser of the Divine Sign, which would ennoble his life by inspiring him with respect for his soul and body, is wearied with the ways of trifling and iniquity, what does he do? Alas! He but too often throws down life as an insupportable burden.

Regarding himself as a beast, for which there is neither fear nor hope beyond the grave, he kills himself. Here, my good Frederic, how can I express to you my sorrow? That which the apostle, ravished with admiration, said of the marvels of heaven,—that eye hath not seen, nor ear heard, nor hath it entered into the heart of man to conceive,—we must now say with fear, shame, and trembling. No; at no epoch, in no climate, among no nation, not even pagans or cannibals, has man ever seen or heard, or his mind conceived, what we see, hear, and touch with our hands. What is it? Suicide. Suicide on a scale without example in history. In France alone, one hundred thousand within the last thirty years! One hundred thousand! And they continue still to increase!

Now, I am almost certain, without having the proof, that of those one hundred thousand persons who died in despair, more than ninety-nine thousand had lost the custom of making the Sign of the Cross frequently, seriously, and religiously. Hold this for the thirteenth article of your Creed. More to-morrow.

Mgr. J.J. Gaume

Sixth Letter

Continuation of the preceding letter—The Sign of the Cross is a book which instructs us—Creation, Redemption, Glorification: three words which contain all the science of God, of man, and of the world—The Sign of the Cross says these three words with authority, with clearness, with sublimity—It says them to every one, everywhere, and always

December 1st

My Dear Frederic,

A Divine Sign, the distinctive mark of the *élite* of humanity, the escutcheon (coat-of-arms) of the Catholic; such, my dear Frederic, is the Sign of the Cross, considered in its first point of view. If it be true that rank imposes obligation, I know of no means more simple, easy, and efficacious to inspire men with sentiments of dignity and respect for themselves, than the Sign of the Cross made frequently, seriously, and religiously. This is one of the reasons of its being.

"This Sign," says a Father of the Church, "is a powerful protection. It is gratuitous, because of the poor; easy, because of the weak. A benefit from God, the standard of the faithful, the terror of demons; far from causing you to despise it, its being a free gift should even increase your gratitude." [S. Cyril, Hier., *Catech.* xiii.] I add, that its eloquence is equal to its power.

What does it say to man? We shall see. *We are ignorant; the Sign of the Cross is a book which instructs us.* Creation, Redemption, Glorification; all science, theological, philosophical, social, political, historical, divine and human, is comprised in these three words. The science of the past, present and future, is here, and here only. These three words are the lights of the world, the bases of intelligence; suppose, for a moment, that the world forgets them, or loses their sense,

~ 51 ~

what does it become? An agglomeration of atoms, moving in empty space, without direction or aim. It becomes blind without guide or staff; an inexplicable mystery to itself; unhappy, without consolation; a galley-slave without hope:— behold man, behold society!

These three words, Creation, Redemption, Glorification, are, then, more necessary to the human race than the bread which nourishes it, or the air that it breathes. They are necessary to every one, at every hour and always. They alone direct a life and every life, an action and every action, a word and every word, a thought and every thought, a joy and every joy, a sadness and every sadness, a sentiment and every sentiment. This supposed, reason says that God owed it to Himself to establish a means, universal, easy, and permanent, by which to give to all that fundamental knowledge; to give it not once, and for a time only, but to renew it unceasingly, as He renews, at every instant, the air which we breathe.

To what doctor shall be given the charge of this indispensable teaching? To St. Paul, St. Augustine, St. Thomas, or any other great genius of the East or the West? No, those doctors die, and we must have one that is immortal. Those doctors dwell in a certain place, and we must have one that lives everywhere. They speak a language that cannot be understood by all; we must have one who speaks intelligibly to every one, to the savage inhabitants of Oceanica, as well as to the civilized inhabitants of the old world. Who, then, shall be our teacher? You know it; it is the Sign of the Cross. It, and it only, fulfils all the requisite conditions. It never dies; it dwells everywhere; its language is universal. In an instant it can give its lesson; in an instant every one can understand it.

In proof of what I assert, allow me, dear friend, to discover a mystery to you. The Incarnate Word, whom Isaias with reason calls the Teacher of mankind, had resolved to die for us. Many kinds of death were presented to Him; stoning, decapitation, poison, being thrown from a high place, fire, water, and what not? Amongst all these, why did He choose the Cross? A learned theologian answered this question many centuries ago. "One of the reasons why Infinite Wisdom has chosen the Cross, is because a slight motion of the hand is sufficient to trace upon us the instrument of the divine torture: bright and powerful Sign, which teaches us all that we have to know, and serves as a buckler against our enemies." [Alcuin, De divin. Office. c. xviii.]

Behold the Sign of the Cross duly established as the catechist of mankind! Is it true, you ask, that it performs its functions well? In other words, that it repeats, and repeats in a becoming manner, the three great words, Creation, Redemption, Glorification? Not only does it repeat them, but it explains them with an authority, sublimity, and clearness which belong to it alone.

With authority—divine in its origin, it is the organ of God Himself. With sublimity and clearness—this you shall see presently. When you place your hand on your forehead while saying, "In the *name*," using only the singular number, the Sign of the Cross teaches you the indivisible unity of the Divine Essence. By this word alone, be you a child or servant-maid, you know more than all the philosophers of paganism. What progress in a single, momentary act! In saying, *of the Father,* what a new and immense ray of light in your intellect! The Sign of the Cross has told you that there is a Being, the Father of all fathers, the Eternal Principle of being, from whom proceed all creatures, celestial and terrestrial, visible and invisible. [Ephes. 3:15] At this new word are dissipated the thick mists which during twenty centuries concealed from the eyes of the pagan world the origin of all things.

You continue to say—*and of the Son*. The adorable sign also continues its teaching. It tells you that the Father of all fathers has a Son like Himself. While making you carry your hand to your breast, when you pronounce His Name, it teaches you that this Eternal Son of God became in time the Son of man, in the womb of a Virgin, in order to redeem man. Man is then fallen.

What brilliant light does this third word cause to rise upon your intellect! The coexistence of good and evil on the earth, the terrible duality which you feel within yourself, that mixture of noble instincts and base propensities, of sublime actions and shameful ones, the necessity of struggling, the possibility and means of rehabilitation, all those mysteries whose depth so long puzzled and perplexed the pagan philosophers, are no longer veiled from you.

You conclude by saying—*and of the Holy Ghost*. This word completes the teachings of the Sign of the Cross. Thanks to it, you know that there is in God, Unity of Essence and Trinity of Persons. You have a just idea of the Being by excellence, the complete Being. He would not be such, were He not one and three. If the First Person is necessarily Power, the Second necessarily Wisdom, the Third is necessarily Love. This Love, essentially beneficent, completes the work of the Father who creates, and of the Son who redeems; He sanctifies man and conducts him to glory.

What clear teaching for the direction of the life of nations and individuals; for kings as well as for subjects! If Aristotle, Plato, Cicero, or any of those ancient seekers after truth; those philosophers, legislators, and moralists exhausted by study and tormented by insolvable doubts, had heard of a master who taught with the depth and sublimity of the Sign of the Cross, we may hold it as certain that they would have gone to the uttermost end of the world to see him, happy to spend their lives in listening to him.

In pronouncing the name of the Holy Ghost, you have formed the Cross. You know not only the Redeemer, but the instrument of Redemption. Thus, while the Sign of the Cross inundates the mind with dazzling lights, it also opens in the heart an inexhaustible source of love; a new benefit, of which I shall speak hereafter.

In the meantime, answer me—Is it possible to teach, in fewer words, with greater eloquence, and in more intelligible language, the three great dogmas of Creation, Redemption, and Glorification, the pivots of the moral world, the generating principles of the human intellect?

A being created, a being destined for eternal glory, a being redeemed;—man, behold what you are!

What do you think of this, dear friend—is not this theology? But if theology is the science of God, of man, and of the world; if philosophy, the rational knowledge of God, of man, and of the world, is the daughter of theology; if from theology and philosophy flow all sciences, politics, ethnics, and history; it follows from this, that the Sign of the Cross is the most learned and the least diffuse doctor that has ever taught.

Do you wish to know what place it holds in the world? I will tell you to-morrow.

Mgr. J.J. Gaume

Seventh Letter

The place which the Sign of the Cross holds in the world—What the human race was before it knew how to make the Sign of the Cross—What becomes of the world when it ceases to make it—Another point of view—The Sign of the Cross is a treasure that enriches us

December 2nd

Dear Friend,

They who despise or contemn the Sign of the Cross have very little suspicion of the place it holds in the world. They belong to that class of persons so numerous in our day, *who suspect nothing, because they doubt nothing.*

Lay aside, for a moment, your office of judge; give me your hand; let us make a brief tour through the ancient and modern worlds. Let us visit first, the brilliant ages of antiquity, in which men knew not how to make the Sign of Cross; and, pilgrims of truth, let us travel through the East and the West.

Memphis, Athens, Rome, three great centres of light, call us to the schools of their wise men.

What say those illustrious masters on the points most important for us to know?

Is the world eternal, or has it been created? If created, by whom was it created? Is the author of nature matter or spirit?

Is he eternal, free, independent?

Are there many?

Answer: Hesitation, uncertainty, flagrant contradictions.

What is good? What is evil? What is their origin? How comes it that they are found in man and in the world?

Is there a remedy for evil, or is it incurable? What is the remedy? Who possesses it? How can we obtain it, how apply it?

Answer: Hesitation, uncertainty, flagrant contradictions.

What is man? Has he a soul? Of what nature is that soul? Is it a fire? A breath? A spirit? Aeriform matter? Is it subject to fate? If it survives the body, what is its destiny? What is the end of its existence?

To all these questions, and to a thousand others, the answer is,—Hesitation, uncertainty, flagrant contradictions.

Ah! Pretended great men and great nations, who cannot give the first word of answer to these fundamental questions— you are but great ignoramuses. What matters it to us that you can invent systems; sharpen sophisms; overwhelm the schools, the senate, and the Areopagus with your inexhaustible eloquence; drive chariots in the circus, build cities; join in battles, conquer provinces, make land and sea tributary to your concupiscence? As long as you are ignorant of what you are, whence you came, and whither you are going, you are, to use the expression of one of your own, *Epicuri de grege porci* (but fattened swine of the herds of Epicurus). Such was the world before the Sign of the Cross.

But this eloquent Sign has appeared.

All those disgraceful darknesses have been dissipated. By making it, man, whether learned or illiterate, has learned the science of himself, of the world, and of God. By repeating it unceasingly, he has engraven it in the very depths of his soul, in such a manner that he can never forget it. Whatever people may say, it was owing to the frequent use of the Sign of the Cross, in all classes of society, in the city as well as in the country, that the Catholic world of the primitive and middle ages, preserved in a degree unknown either before or since, the divine science, the mother of all others, and the light of life.

Could it be otherwise? Let a man during forty years repeat

seriously, ten times a day, any error, whatever it may be, he will end by being completely imbued and identified with it. Why should not the same happen with the truth?

Do you desire the proof of what I advance? Let us continue our journey; come with me through the modern world. It has abandoned the Sign of the Cross. Hence it no longer has a monitor ever at its side to repeat at every instant those three great dogmas so necessary to its moral life. It forgets them; they are for it as if they were not. Now, see what becomes of it with regard to science. Like the ancient world, you hear it stammer shamefully over the very elementary principles of religion, of right, of the family, and of propriety. What grounds of truth maintain its conversations? What are contained in its books of politics and philosophy? By the glimmer of what light does it direct its private life?

And the newspapers, those new Fathers of the Church, what do you think of them? Among the torrent of words which they every day pour out on society, how many sound ideas regarding God, man, or the world, do you find?

What does it know, this modern world, this age of enlightenment, which knows no longer how to make the Sign of the Cross? Neither more nor less than the pagans, its masters and models. The god of self, the god of commerce, the god of cotton, the god of the dollar, *deus venter* (the god of the belly). It knows and adores the goddess of industry, the goddess of steam, the goddess of electricity. As means to satisfy its cupidity, it knows and adores the science of matter, chemistry, physics, mechanism, dynamics, salts, essences, sulphates, nitrates and carbonates. Behold its gods, its worship, its theology, its philosophy, its politics, its morals, its life.

Yet a little more improvement and it will know as much as the contemporaries of Noah, condemned to perish by the waters of the deluge.

For them, also, all science consisted in knowing and adoring the gods of the modern world; in drinking, eating, building, buying, selling, marrying, and being married. Man had concentrated his life in matter. He had become flesh, ignorant as flesh, foul as flesh. [St. Matt. 24:37-39. St. Luke 17:28. Gen. 6:12 Ibid. 3.]

Of all those inclinations, which is wanting to the world of our day? Although less advanced than that of the giants, is it not of the same nature? As for the rest, nothing better can be expected from it. Knowing no longer how to make the Sign of the Cross, or refusing to make it, it materializes itself, and in virtue of the law of moral gravitation, falls back into the state in which it was before it knew how to make it.

We are ignorant; the Sign of the Cross is a book which instructs us. From this new point of view, you can judge whether our forefathers were wrong in making it incessantly.

That the deplorable ignorance of the present world may, in a great measure, be ascribed to its abandonment of the Sign of the Cross, you shall presently see.

What is ignorance? Ignorance is poverty of the mind. In matters of religion it is more frequently called poverty of the heart. Poverty of the heart comes from its weakness in practicing virtue and rejecting evil. Why this weakness? Because man neglects the means of obtaining grace, or rendering it efficacious. The first, the most familiar, prompt and easy of those means, is, as you know, prayer. Of all prayers, the easiest, shortest, most familiar, and perhaps the most powerful, is the Sign of the Cross. A new meditation for you, a new justification for the early Christians.

We are poor; the Sign of the Cross is a treasure that enriches us. A beggar is one who goes daily from door to door to beg his bread. Croesus was a beggar, Alexander was a beggar, Cæsar was a beggar, all emperors and kings, all empresses and queens were beggars; crowned beggars indeed, but always beggars.

Who is the man, no matter how opulent we may suppose him to be, who is not obliged to say every day at the door of the great Father of the family, *Give us this day our daily bread*?

Can the most potent monarch make a grain of wheat? Man has received everything, physical and moral life, and the means of preserving both, *quid habes quod non accepisti* (what hast thou that thou hast not received)? [1 Corinthians IV, 7] He possesses nothing of his own, not even one hair of his head.

Again, what he has received, has not been given him once for all. He is in want every day, every hour, every instant. If God, the giver of all, were to withhold His gifts for a moment, man should die. Since then man has nothing, and is in want of everything, at every instant he must beg.

From this, my dear Frederic, arises a great law of the moral world, on which, most certainly, your young companions have never reflected. I mean the law of prayer.

The pagans of the ancient world, the idolaters and savages of the present day have lost more or less of the patrimony of traditionary truths, but none have lost their knowledge of the law of prayer. Man, from his first appearance on the globe, has invariably observed it under one form or another.

Stronger than all passions, more eloquent than all sophisms, the instinct of self-preservation told him that on his invariable fidelity to it depended his existence: it did not deceive him. On that day, on which no prayer, either human or angelic, would be raised to God, all relations would cease between the Creator and the creature, between the Giver and the beggar; and the flow of the river of life would, at that instant, be suspended.

Is not this the profound mystery revealed to the world by the Incarnate Word Himself, when He said: *Oportet semper orare et nunquam deficere* (that we ought always to pray, and not to faint)? [St. Luke XVIII, 1] Take notice how imperative are these words. The law-giver does not invite; He commands, and the commandment is of absolute necessity, *oportet*; He allows of no intermission, either day or night, in the accomplishment of the law, *oportet semper*. As long as man shall be a beggar in the sight of God, so long shall the law of prayer never be modified, never recalled, never suspended; and as man must always be a mendicant, it follows that the law of prayer shall preserve its empire unto the last day of the world: *et nunquam deficere*. The physical world itself has been organized with reference to the perpetual observance of this conserving law of the moral world. Thanks to the successive passage of the sun over one hemisphere or the other, one-half of mankind are always awake for prayer.

Now, one of the most powerful prayers is the Sign of the Cross. All mankind have believed this. They believed it only because they had learned it; they could have learned it only from God Himself, from whom they have learned everything. I say *all mankind*, designedly. Your young companions believe, perhaps, that the Sign of the Cross dates from Christianity, or that, at least, its use has been limited to the Jews and Catholics. In my next letter I will show you what confidence this opinion deserves.

Mgr. J.J. Gaume

Eighth Letter

The Sign of the Cross known and practiced since the beginning of the world—Contradictions only apparent—Seven ways of making the Sign of the Cross—Testimonies of the Fathers—David, Solomon, and all the Jewish nation made the Sign of the Cross, and knew its value

December 3rd

My Dear Frederic,

Your ears and those of many others will tingle at the first sentence of my letter—the Sign of the Cross runs back to the very beginning of the world. It has been made by all nations, even by pagans, in their solemn prayers on important occasions, when they desired to obtain some signal favors. Let me first remark, that between this proposition and that which I advanced in my preceding letter, there is no contradiction. Yesterday I spoke of the Sign of the Cross in its perfect form and fully understood, such as we practice it since the Gospel. To-day I speak of the Sign of the Cross in a form, elementary though real, and more or less mysterious to those who made it before the Gospel. An explanation seems to be necessary. I am about to give it.

The Sign of the Cross is so natural to man, that at no epoch, among no nation, and in no form of worship, did man ever put himself in communication with God by prayer, without making the Sign of the Cross. Do you know of any nation who were accustomed to pray with their arms hanging down? As for me, I do not. All those that I know, and I know the Jews, the Pagans, and the Catholics, have, in prayer, made the Sign of the Cross.

There are seven ways of making it:

With the arms extended: man then becomes an entire Sign of

the Cross.

With hands clasped, the fingers interlaced, thus forming five Signs of the Cross.

The hands joined, one against the other, the thumbs placed one over the other; again the Sign of the Cross.

The hands crossed on the breast; another form of the Sign of the Cross.

The arms equally crossed on the breast; fifth way of making it.

The thumb of the right hand passing under the index finger and resting on the middle one; a Sign of the Cross much in use, as we shall see hereafter.

And finally, the right hand passing from the forehead to the breast, and from the breast to the shoulders; a more explicit form, which you know.

Under one or other of these forms, the Sign of the Cross has been practiced everywhere and always, in solemn circumstances, with a knowledge more or less clear of its efficacy.

Jacob lies at the point of death. Around him stand his twelve sons, the future fathers of the twelve tribes of Israel. Inspired by God, the holy patriarch announces to each what shall happen to him in succeeding ages. At the sight of Ephraim and Manasses, Joseph's two children, the old man being moved, invokes on them all the blessings of heaven. To obtain them what does he do? He crosses his arms, says the Scripture, and places his left hand on the child at his right, and his right on the one at his left. Behold the Sign of the Cross, the eternal token of benediction!

In this, tradition is not deceived. Jacob was the type of the Messiah. In that solemn moment, words, attitude, everything in the patriarch was prophetic.

"Jacob," says St. John of Damascus, "in crossing his hands to bless Joseph's children, forms the Sign of the Cross; nothing is more evident." [De Fib. orthod., lib. iv. c. 12.]

Even from apostolic times, Tertullian established the same fact, and gave it the like meaning. "The Old Testament," says he, "shows us Jacob blessing Joseph's children, his left hand passed over on the head of him at his right, and the right on the head of him at his left. In this position they formed the Sign of the Cross, and foretold the blessings of which the Crucified should be the source." [De Baptism.]

Let us go back to the time of the servitude in Egypt, and pass on to Moses. Having reached the midst of the desert, the Hebrews find themselves face to face with Amalec. At the head of a powerful army, the hostile king stops their passage. A decisive battle is inevitable. What will Moses do? Instead of remaining in the plain, to encourage, by his voice and gesture, the battalions of Israel, he ascends the mountain which commands a view of the battle-field. What does the lawgiver, inspired by God, do during the combat? He makes the Sign of the Cross, nothing but the Sign of the Cross, and the Sign of the Cross during the whole of the combat. Nowhere do we learn that he pronounces any words. With hands open, and arms extended toward heaven, he makes himself a living Sign of the Cross. God sees him in this attitude, and the victory is gained. [Exod. xvii. 10.]

This is not an idle supposition. Listen again to the Fathers of the Church. "Amalec," cries out St. John of Damascus, "those hands extended in the form of a Cross, have vanquished thee!" [De Fid. orthod., lib. iv. c. 12.] And the great Tertullian: "Why does Moses, at the time that Joshua is about to combat with Amalec, do what he never did before—pray with extended arms? In a circumstance so decisive, should he not, in order to render his prayer more efficacious, bend his knee, strike his breast, and bow his head to the dust? Nothing of all this. Why? Because that combat of the Lord in which Amalec was delivered up a prey, prefigured the battles of the Incarnate Word against satan, and the Sign of the Cross, by which He was to conquer." [Contr. Marcian., bib. III.]

And St. Justin, the philosopher and martyr, who lived so near the time of the apostles, says: "Moses with extended arms, upheld by Hur and Aaron, remaining on the mountain until sunset, what is he but a living Sign of the Cross?" [Dialog. cum Tryph., n. iii.]

Insensible to the miracles of the paternal solicitude, of which they were the constant objects, the Hebrews murmur against Moses and against God. Murmurs rise to revolt, and the revolt becomes general and obstinate. The chastisement is not long delayed, and it assumes the same characteristics. Royal serpents, frightful reptiles whose venom burns like fire, fall upon the guilty and wound them with their fangs. The camp is filled with the dead and dying. At the prayer of Moses, God shows them mercy. To put the serpents to flight and heal the innumerable sick, what means will He indicate? Prayers? No. Fasts? No. An altar? An expiatory column? Nothing of all this. He orders him to make a Sign of the Cross, permanent and visible to all; a sign that each of the sick shall make in his heart, only by looking at it, and such shall be the power of this sign, that one look alone shall suffice to restore him to health. The signification of this divinely commanded sign is not doubtful. The true Sign of the Cross, the eternally living Sign of the Cross, Our Lord Himself, has revealed to mankind that the sign of the desert was a figure of Himself. "And as Moses lifted up the serpent in the desert, so must the Son of man be lifted up; that whosoever believeth in him may not perish, but may have life everlasting." [St. John 3:15]

If the limits of a letter permitted, we might read together the annals of this typical people, and you would see, my dear friend, that on all important occasions, the only ones which we know well, they had recourse to the Sign of the Cross. I will cite a few of them. In the sacrifices, the priest first raised the victim in the manner prescribed by law. He then carried it from east to west, as we learn from the Jews themselves; thus was made the Sign of the Cross. It was by the same motion that the high-priest, and even the simple priests, blessed the people after the sacrifice. [Duquet. Treat. of the Cross of Our Lord, c. viii.]

From the Jewish Church, this sign passed to the Christian. The first faithful, struck by the ancient manner of blessing with the Sign of the Cross, were easily instructed by the apostles on its mysterious signification, and naturally inclined to continue it, adding the divine words which explain it.

In the time of the prophet Ezechiel the abominations of Jerusalem were at their height. A mysterious personage, says the prophet, received orders to traverse the city, and to mark the sign T on the foreheads of all those who mourned over the abominations of that guilty capital. By his side walked six other persons, each armed with a deadly weapon, who were commanded to kill indiscriminately all those not marked with the salutary sign. [Ezech. 9:4, etc.]

How is it possible not to see here a striking figure of the Sign of the Cross which is made on our foreheads? Thus it is understood by the Fathers of the Church, among others, by

Tertullian and St. Jerome. "As," say they, "the sign *Thau* (**T**) marked on the foreheads of the inhabitants of Jerusalem, who grieved over the crimes of that city, protected them against the exterminating angel, so also the Sign of the Cross, marked on the forehead of a man, is an assurance that he shall not become the victim of the demon and the other enemies of his salvation, if he really grieve over the abomination which this sign interdicts." [Tertull., adv. Marcion., lib. iii. c. 22; S. Hier. in Ezech. c. x.]

The Philistines have reduced the Israelites to the most humiliating servitude. Samson begins their deliverance, but, unhappily, the strength of Israel allows himself to be surprised. They load him with chains, after having caused his eyes to be pulled out. They make a plaything of him, to amuse them at their feasts. Samson, however, meditates revenge. He plans how, with one blow, he may be able to destroy thousands of enemies.

Providence has so arranged things that it is by the Sign of the Cross he shall consummate his design. "Placed between two pillars that support the edifice," says St. Augustine, "the Strength of Israel extends his arms in the form of a cross. In this all-powerful attitude, he shakes the pillars; they give way, he crushes his enemies; and like the Great Crucified, of whom he is the figure, he dies, buried in his own triumph." [Serm. 107, de Temp.]

David, overwhelmed with sorrow, is reduced to the greatest extremity in which a king can find himself. A parricidal son, revolting subjects, and unsteady throne, old age fast coming on! What does the inspired monarch do? He prays, by making the Sign of the Cross. [Expandi manus meas ad te (I stretched out my hands to thee). Ps. 83, 142, etc., etc.]

Solomon finishes the temple of Jerusalem. The magnificent

edifice is consecrated with a pomp worthy of the monarch. He wishes to draw down the blessings of heaven upon the new dwelling of the God of Israel, and to obtain His favors for those who will come there to pray. What does Solomon do? He prays, by making the Sign of the Cross. "And Solomon," says the Sacred Text, "stood before the altar of the Lord, in the sight of the assembly of Israel, and spread forth his hands toward heaven, and said: Lord God of Israel, there is no God like Thee in heaven above, or on earth beneath.   .   .   .   Have regard to the prayer of Thy servant.   .   .   .   That Thy eyes may be opened on this house night and day;   .   .   .   That Thou mayest hearken to the supplication of Thy servant, and of Thy people Israel." [III Kings 8:22. et seq.]

To believe that the patriarchs, judges, and prophets, the kings and the seers of Israel were the only ones who knew and practiced the Sign of the Cross, would be an error. All the people knew it, and in times of public danger made religious use of it.

Sennacherib is advancing from victory to victory. The greater part of Palestine is invaded; Jerusalem itself is threatened. Behold what that entire nation, men, women, and children, do to repulse the enemy. Like Moses, they make the Sign of the Cross; become living images of that holy sign. "And they invoked the Lord of mercies, and spreading their hands, they lifted them up to heaven. And the Lord quickly heard them." [Eccl. 48:2.]

Another danger threatens them. Heliodorus, with a numerous band of soldiers, comes to pillage the Temple. He has already entered the exterior enclosure; yet a few moments and the sacrilege shall be consummated. The Priests lie prostrate at the foot of the altar, but nothing stops the spoliator.

What do the people do? They have recourse to their traditional weapon; they pray, making the Sign of the Cross. You know the rest. [II Machab. 3:20.]

If it is incontestable that to pray with outstretched arms is one form of the Sign of the Cross, you see that from all antiquity the Jews have known and practiced it, with a mysterious instinctive feeling of its power. We shall see to-morrow if the pagans were much less instructed.

Mgr. J.J. Gaume

Ninth Letter

The Sign of the Cross among Pagans—New details of an exterior form of the Sign of the Cross among the first Christians—The Martyrs in the amphitheatre—Etymology of the word *adore*—The Pagans adored by making the Sign of the Cross—How they made it—First manner

December 4th

My Dear Frederic,

The Sign of the Cross among the pagans; such, my friend, is the subject of this letter. In order to follow to the end the traditional chain which unites the synagogue to the church, I am going to say a word to you about the Sign of the Cross among the primitive Christians. You are already aware that they made it at every instant, but are, perhaps, ignorant, that in order not to interrupt it while they were praying, they transformed themselves into Signs of the Cross. In any case, I would wager a hundred against one, that your companions know nothing of it.

What Moses, Samson, David, and the Israelites did only at intervals, our forefathers did always; you will understand the reason of this. Amalec, the Philistines, Heliodorus, were passing enemies, while the Roman giant never laid down his arms. Between our fathers and him the struggle was continual; it was carried to the extreme; it was without respite or intermission.

Under those circumstances each became as another Moses on the Mount. Not for one day, but during three centuries did their hands remain extended towards heaven, asking, like those of the Hebrew law-giver, victory for the martyrs in the arena, and the conversion of their persecutors.

Let us hear an eye-witness speak of their thoughts and

attitude in prayer. "We pray," says Tertullian, "with our eyes raised toward heaven, and our hands outstretched, because they are innocent; our heads bare, because we have nothing to blush for; without a monitor, because we pray from the heart. In this attitude we unceasingly implore that all the emperors may have a long life, a peaceful reign, a palace free from snares, a valorous army, a virtuous people, a tranquil world; in a word, for all the wishes of the man and the Cæsar. [Apol., c. xxx.]

Thus prayed, in the East and the West, men, women, children, young men, young virgins, old men, senators, matrons, the faithful of all conditions. This mysterious attitude they kept not only in their meetings in the depths of the catacombs, in pleading the interests of others, but they also took it with them, when, dragged into the amphitheatre, they had to fight for themselves, under the eyes of innumerable spectators, the great combat of martyrdom. Can you, my dear friend, imagine a more affecting spectacle than that of which Eusebius gives us a description?

The persecution of Diocletian was raging with great violence in Phoenicia. One day a great number of Christians, condemned to the wild beasts, were to be seen entering the amphitheatre. The spectators shuddered with deep emotion at the sight of that multitude of children, youths, and old men, stripped of their garments, their eyes raised to heaven, their arms extended in the form of a Cross, standing immovable, without fear or surprise, in the midst of ravenous lions and tigers. The fear, which ought to have agitated the condemned, had passed into the souls of the spectators, and even of the judges." [Hist. eccl., lib. viii., c. 5.]

That attitude was not exceptional. Let us listen again to the same historian; none is more worthy of credit, for he was an eye-witness of what he relates. "You should have seen in the midst of the amphitheatre," says he, "a young man not yet twenty years of age, freed from his bonds, standing tranquilly, his arms extended in the form of a Cross, his eyes and heart fixed on heaven, praying with fervor, motionless in the midst of bears and leopards, whose fury threatened instant death; then those furious beasts, ready to tear his flesh, suddenly muzzled, as it were, by a mysterious power, hastily fled away." [Hist. eccl., lib. viii. c. 7.]

On account of the delicacy of the victim, the West offers us a still more affecting sight. It was in the midst of the great city of Rome. Never had such multitudes crowded the steps of the circus. The heroine was Agnes, a noble virgin only thirteen years old. Condemned to the fire, she ascends the funeral pile.

"Do you see her," says St. Ambrose, "stretching her hands towards Christ, and even in the midst of the flames erecting the victorious standard of the Lord? With hands outstretched through the flames, she offers to God the following prayer: O Thou Whom we must adore, honor, and fear: Almighty Father of Our Lord Jesus Christ, I bless Thee, because, thanks to Thine only Son, I have escaped from the hands of impious men, and have passed unsullied through the impurities of the demon. And behold, moreover, that by the dew of the Holy Ghost is extinguished the fire which surrounds me; the flames are divided, and the burning heat of my pile threatens those who have enkindled it." [Lib. I. de Virgin.]

Such was the eloquent form of the Sign of the Cross in use among the Christians of the primitive Church, those Moseses of the new covenant. You may see another proof of this on the paintings in the Catacombs. This form has lasted a long time. I saw it practiced about thirty years ago, by some of the German people. But even if this form be in disuse among the faithful, the Church religiously preserves it. The two hundred thousand priests who every day ascend the altar, in every part of the globe, are the visible links of that traditional chain which extends from us to the Catacombs, from the Catacombs to Calvary, from Calvary to Raphidim, and then is lost in the night of time.

Let us speak of the pagans. They also made the Sign of the Cross. They made it in prayer, and, with good reason, believed it to be endued with mysterious strength of great importance. Ask your companions for the etymology of the word *adorare* (adore). They will not be at a loss for the answer. If this word were a creation of the Church, you might dispense yourself from asking the question, but it is found in the Latin of the Golden Age, as they say in colleges, and they, bachelors just fresh from college, ought to know it.

Analyzing it, then, we find that the infinitive verb, *to adore*, signifies, according to all etymologists, *manum ad os admovere* (to bring the hand to the mouth and kiss it). Such was the way in which the pagans honored their gods. Proofs of this abound.

"When we adore," says Pliny, "we bring our right hand to our mouth and kiss it; then we describe a circle with our body, we turn ourselves around."*

Hear Minutius Felix: "Cecilius saw the statue of Serapis, and, according to the custom of the superstitious people, put his hand to his mouth and kissed it." [In Octav.]

Apuleius: "Until now Æmilianus has prayed to no god; he has frequented no temple. If he passes before a sacred place, he regards it as a crime to bring his hand to his lips to adore." [Apol. I., vers. fin.]

Why did this gesture express the sovereign worship, the worship of adoration? I will tell you in two words. Man is the image of God. God is entire in His Word; by Him He does all things. Like God, man is entire in his word; it is by it that he does everything. To carry the hand to the mouth, is to repress the word; it is, in some sort, to be annihilated.

To do it as the pagans did, to honor the demon, was to declare themselves his vassals, his subjects, his slaves, and even to acknowledge him as god. You see that it was an enormous crime. Hence the remarkable words of Job, pleading his cause: "If I beheld the sun when it shined, and the moon advancing in brightness; and my heart in secret hath rejoiced, and I have

---

* Hist. Nat., lib. xxviii. NOTE—"We turn ourselves around." What means this kind of adoration? By carrying the hand to the mouth, man pays the homage of his person to the divinity; by turning around, he imitates the motion of the planets, and offers to the divinity the homage of the whole world, of which the celestial bodies are the most noble portion. This manner of adoring was a part of Sabianism, or the worship of the stars, which dates back to the farthest antiquity. According to the Pythagoreans, this form had come from Numa, who prescribed the turning around; *Circumage te cum deos adoras.* "It is said," adds Plutarch, "that it is a representation of the revolution which the heavens make in their motion." This profoundly mysterious practice was wide-spread in America, before its discovery; it is still in use among the turning dervishes in the East.

kissed my hand with my mouth: which is a very great iniquity, and a denial against the most high God." [Job, xxxi, 26-28.]

This mysterious gesture was so particular a sign of idolatry, that in speaking of the Israelites who had remained faithful, God said: "And I will leave me seven thousand men in Israel whose knees have not been bowed before Baal, and every mouth that hath not worshipped him, kissing the hands." [3 Kings, 19:18.]

The pagans adored by carrying the hand to the mouth and kissing it: the fact is incontestable; but you will tell me that in all this you do not see the Sign of the Cross. You shall see it presently, in the manner of kissing the hand.

Look at that pagan, his knee bent to the ground, or his head bowed before his idols. Do you see him passing the thumb of his right hand under the index, and resting it on the middle finger, so as to form a cross; then devoutly kissing that cross, murmuring a few words in honor of his gods? Repeat the gesture yourself, and you will see that the Sign of the Cross could not be better formed.

That such was the manner of the adoring kiss among many other pagans, we learn from Apuleius: "A multitude of citizens and strangers," says he, "were attracted by the noise of the ravishing spectacle. Amazed at the admirable beauty of which they were the witnesses, they carried their right hand to their mouth, the index resting on the thumb; and by religious prayers honored it even as the divinity." [Asin. Aur., lib. iv. As to the accompanying murmur, see Ovid vi., Metamorph. Restilit et pavido, faveas murmure dixit Dux mens: et simili, faveas mihi, murmure dixi.]

This manner of making the Sign of the Cross is so true and so expressive, that it remains, even in our day, familiar to a great number of Christians in every country. It was not the only one known to the pagans. Such of them as were the most pious, made the Sign of the Cross by joining their hands over the breast. We find this Sign of the Cross in one of the most solemn and mysterious circumstances of their public life. I leave your curiosity unsatisfied until to-morrow.

Mgr. J.J. Gaume

Tenth Letter

Second and third way in which the Pagans made the Sign of the Cross—Testimonies—The *Pietas publica*—The Pagans acknowledged a mysterious power in the Sign of the Cross— Whence came that belief—Great mystery of the moral world— Importance of the Sign of the Cross in the sight of God—The Sign of the Cross in the physical world—Words of the Fathers and of Plato—Inconsistency of the ancient and modern Pagans—Reason of the especial hatred of the demon for the Sign of the Cross

December 4th

My Dear Frederic,

Coming out of college after ten years of Greek and Latin studies, we do not know the first word of pagan antiquity. Education continually shows us the upper side of the cards, but never the under side. What happens in France, I have reason to believe, happens also among our neighbors. Hence it comes, my dear friend, that the fact with which I am about to entertain you, will be for many a strange novelty. Here it is.

When a Roman army began to lay siege to a city, the first operation of the general, whoever he might be, whether Camillus, Fabius, Metellus, Cæsar, or Scipio, was not to dig trenches, or raise lines of circumvallation, but to evoke the gods, the defenders of the city, and to call them into his camp. The formula of evocation is too long for a letter; you will find it in Macrobius.

Now then, in pronouncing it, the general made the Sign of the Cross twice; first as did Moses and the early Christians, and as the priest does now at the altar. With hands extended towards heaven, he pronounced in supplication the name of Jupiter. Then, full of confidence in the efficacy of his prayer, he devoutly crossed his hands upon his breast. [Satur., lib. iii. c. 2.]

Behold here the Sign of the Cross under two forms, incontestable, universal, and perfectly regular.

If this remarkable fact is generally ignored, there is another a little less so. The custom of praying with outstretched arms was familiar to the pagans of the East and West. On this point there is no difference between them, the Jews, and ourselves. Read your classics over again.

Livy says to you: "On their knees, they raised their suppliant hands to heaven, and to the gods." [Lib. xxxvi.]

Dionysius of Halicarnassus: "Brutus, hearing of the misfortune and death of Lucretia, raised his hands to heaven, and invoked Jupiter and all the gods." [Antiquit. lib. iv.]

And Virgil: "At Pater Anchises, passis de littare palmis Numina magna vocat (Father Anchises on the shore, his hands raised, invoked the great gods)." [Æneid. lib. iii.]

And Athenæus: "Darius, having heard with what regard Alexander treated his captive daughters, stretched his hands toward the sun, and begged that if he himself were not to reign, the empire might be given to Alexander." [Lib. xiii. c. 27.]

In fine, Apuleius declares formally, that this manner of praying was not an exception, or, as some young moderns would qualify it, *an eccentricity*, but a permanent custom. "The attitude of those who pray," says he, "is to raise the hands to heaven." [Lib. de Mundo. vers fin.]

An instinct, which I will call traditional, for otherwise it would have no name, taught them the value of this mysterious sign. To be able to make it at their last moments was for them an assured pledge of salvation.

"If death," says Arrian, "should surprise me in the midst of my occupations, it will be enough for me that I be able to raise my hands to heaven." [In Epictet., lib. iv. c. 10.]

Take notice, that he does not say: If I can fall on my knees, or strike my breast, or bow my forehead to the dust; but, If I can extend my arms in the form of a cross, and raise them towards heaven. And why this? Ask your companions.

Ask them why the Egyptians placed the cross in their temples, prayed before that adorable sign, and looked upon it as an omen of future happiness. "When, in the time of Theodosius," relate the Greek historians, Socrates and Sozomen, "they were destroying the temples of the false gods, they found that of Serapis, in Egypt, full of stones marked with the Sign of the Cross. This made them say to the neophytes, that between Jesus Christ and Serapis there was something in common. They added, that among them the cross signified the future age." [Socrat., lib. v. c. 17.—Sozom., lib. vii. c. 15.]

Among the Romans this same instinct was transferred by a fact, of which I would be inclined to doubt, did I not have weighty proof of it in an antique medal placed before my eyes. Knowing, on the one side, the efficacy of the Sign of the Cross, which I have described, yet on the other, not being willing, like Moses or the early Christians, to remain with their arms in the form of a cross during all their prayers, what did they do?

They imagined a goddess, commissioned to intercede continually for the republic, and represented her in the attitude of Moses on the Mount. Therefore in Rome, in the centre of the *Forum olitorium* (the lesser forum), where are now to be seen the ruins of the theatre of Marcellus, was raised the statue of the goddess called *Pietas publica* (Public Piety). She is represented standing, with her arms outstretched in the form of a cross, absolutely like Moses on the Mount, or the early Christians in the Catacombs. She has, moreover, at her left an altar, on which burns incense, the symbol of prayer. [Gretzer, De

Cruce, p. 33. Forcellini.]

On the impetratory and adoring value of the Sign of the Cross, the far East agreed with the West, the Chinese with the Romans.

Would you believe that Hien Yuen, an emperor of China, in times so ancient as to be almost mythological, had, like Plato, foreseen the mystery of the Cross?

"To honor the Most High, that ancient emperor joined two pieces of wood together, one straight, the other transverse." [Prelim. Discourse of Chou-king by Premare, ch. ix. p. xcii.]

Thus of the seven ways of making the Sign of the Cross, three were known to the pagans, and practiced religiously by them, particularly on important occasions. All this is very well, you will say, but did they know what they were doing? Was it not a sign purely arbitrary, and therefore insignificant, from which we can draw no conclusions? That the pagans understood the Sign of the Cross as we do, is what I would not pretend to say. It was with them, as with the figures among the Jews. In their eyes it had a real signification, a considerable value, although more or less mysterious, according to the places, times, and persons.

You know of letters written with sympathetic (invisible) ink. At first sight, the characters, although really traced, are scarcely apparent, but when brought near the fire, they immediately appear, and are perfectly legible. Such was the Sign of the Cross among the pagans. When struck with the rays of evangelical light, this *clare-obscure* ("invisible ink") no more changed its nature than did the figures of the Old Testament, but like them it became intelligible to all; it discovered itself, it spoke.

To believe that among the pagans this sign was an arbitrary

one is a supposition that falls of itself. Anything universal is never arbitrary; the Sign of the Cross less so than anything else. Here, my dear Frederic, we touch upon one of the most profound mysteries of the moral order.

Forget not that my present aim is to show in the Sign of the Cross a treasure that enriches us. To be enriched, man must ask, and God must give. In order that God may hear man, man must be agreeable in the sight of God: *Deus peccatores non exaudit* (God doth not hear sinners). [St. John IX, 31] No one is pleasing to God but His Son, and those who are like Him.

Now, the Son of God, the only Mediator between God and man, is a living Sign of the Cross, a sign eternally living, from the beginning of the world: Agnus occisus ab origine mundi (the Lamb which was slain from the beginning of the world). [Apocalypse XIII, 8] He is the great Crucified, and the great Crucified is the new Adam, the type of mankind. In order to be agreeable to God, it is necessary that man should resemble his Divine Model, and be crucified; be a living Sign of the Cross.

Such, like that of the Word Himself, is his destiny upon earth. As a beggar, this is principally the position he must take when he presents himself before God to ask for alms.

Providence has not wished that he should be ignorant of this condition necessary for success. Man has no more lost the knowledge of the instrument of his redemption than of his fall, and his hope in the Redeemer. Hence the existence and practice of the Sign of the Cross in prayer, among all nations, from the beginning of ages even to our own day. God has engraven the instinct of the Sign of the Cross on the heart of man. In order to keep ever-present, even to his corporal eyes, the necessity of this salutary sign, and to make him understand the sovereign part which it must play in the moral world, the Creator has willed that, in the material world everything should be done by this sign, that all in it should show this necessary action and reproduce its image.

Listen to men who had eyes to see.

"It is exceedingly remarkable," says Gretzer, "that, from the very beginning of the world, God has been pleased to keep the figure of the Cross continually before the eyes of mankind, and has so organized things that man can scarcely do anything without the intervention of the Sign of the Cross." [De Cruce, lib. i. c. 52.]

Gretzer is the hundredth echo of traditional philosophy. Listen to others.

"Look," say they, "at everything in the world, and see if all is not governed and put in motion by the Sign of the Cross. The bird that flies in the air, the man that swims in the water, or that offers a prayer, makes the Sign of the Cross, and can act only by it.

"To gain a fortune and to seek riches at the extremity of the world, the navigator needs a ship; the ship cannot sail without a mast, and the mast and the sail-yards form the Cross; without it no government is possible, no fortune is to be hoped for. The husbandman seeks food from the earth, the food of the rich and of kings. To obtain it, he must have a plough. The plough cannot open the earth unless it is armed with the plough-share, and the plough with the plough-share forms the Cross. [S. Hier. in. c. xi. Mark.—Orig., Hamil. viii. in divers—S. Maxim. Pourin., ap. S. Ambr. t. m. serm. 56. etc., etc. We could cite many thousand other applications.]

If this sign is the means by which man acts over nature, it is also the instrument of his actions over his fellow-creatures. In battle, is it not the sight of the flag that animates the soldiers? What do we see on the Roman Cantabra and Siparia of the standards, if not a Cross? Both one and the other were gilded lances, surmounted with a piece of wood placed horizontally, from which depended a veil of purple and gold. The eagles with outspread wings placed on the top of the lances, and the other military insignia always surmounted by two extended wings, invariably remind us of the Sign of the Cross.

The trophies and monuments of victories gained, always formed a Cross. The religion of the Romans was all warlike; they adored their standards, swore by their standards, preferred them to all their gods; and all their standards were crosses: *Omnes illi imaginum suggestus insignes monilia crucium sunt.* [Tertul. Apolog. xvi.]

Therefore when Constantine wished to perpetuate the remembrance of the Cross by which he had vanquished, he was not obliged to change the imperial standard; but contented himself with causing the cipher of Christ to be engraven on it, as if it was only necessary to name Him of whom he had had the vision, and not the object of that vision. [Euseb., lib. ix., Histor. 9.]

Man, in his turn, is distinguished exteriorly from beasts, because he can stand and extend his arms; and man, standing in this posture, forms the Cross. We are also commanded to pray in this attitude, to the end that our members themselves should proclaim the Passion of the Lord. When our soul and body, each after its manner, confess Jesus on the Cross, then it is that our prayers are more speedily granted.

Heaven itself is disposed in the form of the Cross. What do the four cardinal points represent, if not the four arms of the Cross, and the universality of its salutary virtue?

The whole creation bears the impress of the Cross. Has not Plato himself written, that the Power nearest to the first God, is

extended over the world in the form of a Cross? [S. Maxim.—
Taurin. apud S. Amb. t. iii. ser. 56.—3 Hier., In Marc xi.; Tertul., Apol. xvi.—
Origen. Homil. viii. in divers.—S. Just. Apol. ii, etc., etc.]

Hence the peremptory response of Minutius Felix to the
pagans who reproached the Christians for making the Sign of
the Cross. "Is not this cross everywhere?" said he to them.
"Your ensigns, your banners, the standards of your camps,
your trophies—what are they, if not crosses gilded and
ornamented? Do not you, as well as we, pray with extended
arms? In that solemn attitude do you not use formulas by
which you proclaim one only God? Do you not, then, resemble
the Christians, who adore one only God, and have the courage
to confess their faith in the midst of torments, with their arms
extended in the form of a Cross?

"Between you and us what difference is there, when with
your arms outstretched in the form of the cross, you say: 'Great
God, true God, if God wishes?' Is this the natural language of
the pagan, or rather the prayer of the Christian? *Ita signo crucis
aut ratio naturalis innititur, au vestra religio formatur.* (Then
either the Sign of the Cross is the foundation of natural reason,
or it serves as the basis of your religion)." [Octav.]

"Why, then," added some other apologists, "why do you
persecute it?" And I also, my dear Frederic, can address the
same question to the modern pagans. Why do you persecute
the Sign of the Cross? Why are you ashamed of it? Why do
you pursue with your sarcasms those who have the courage to
make it? The answer is the same today as in former times.
Satan, the great ape of God, put himself in competition with the
Sign of the Cross; he permitted the pagans to make it for his
own profit. The perfidious wretch! He was glad to see men
employ for his worship and their own loss, even that sign

destined for the adoration of the true God, and their salvation. As to the Christians, it was otherwise. By them the Sign of the Cross was brought back to its true destination. It honored the true God, and in particular, the Incarnate Word, the object of the personal hatred of satan, from whom He rescued man, his victim; then in the Christian, the Sign of the Cross became an object of raillery, a crime deserving of death. Nothing has changed. Therefore in our day the Sign of the Cross is an object of mockery with the slaves of satan; but when employed in profane uses or occult practices, it provokes neither their hatred or sarcasm. Whence come, then, among the wicked of every age, those dispositions, in appearance so contradictory, of love and hatred, of respect and contempt for this adorable sign? "From satan himself," answers Tertullian. "Spirit of lies, it is his part to alter truth, and turn the most holy things to the profit of idols. He baptizes his faithful, assuring them that water will remit their sins; in this way he imitates the worship of Mithras. He marks his soldiers on the forehead. He celebrates the oblation of the bread. He promises resurrection, and a crown bought by the sword.

"What do I say? He has a sovereign pontiff to whom he forbids a second marriage. He has his virgins; he has his chaste ones. If we examine in detail the superstitions established by Numa, the sacerdotal offices, the insignia, the privileges, the order and detail of the sacrifices, the sacred utensils, even the vessels used for the sacrifices, all the objects employed for expiations and prayers; is it not manifest that the demon, the robber of Moses, has counterfeited all these? And since the Gospel, the imitation still continues. [De prescript.]

Satan goes still further. Knowing all the power of the Sign of the Cross, he has wished to make of it a personal symbol, that by this substitution he may engross all the homage due from the world to the Crucified God.

"Instructed by the prophetic oracles," says Firmicus Maternus, "the implacable enemy of mankind has made that which was established for the salvation of the world, serve as the instrument of iniquity. What are those horns which he boasts of having? The caricature of those of which the inspired prophet of God speaks, and which you, satan, believe you can adapt to your hideous figure. How can you seek in them for ornament and glory? Those horns are but the figure of the venerable Sign of the Cross." [De error. profan. relig. xxii.]

Now the forehead marked with the Sign of the Cross makes him shudder with rage. He finds no torments cruel enough to punish him who bears the image of the Incarnate Word. See, dear friend, how he treats our fathers, our mothers, our brothers, and sisters, the martyrs of all times and all countries. Sometimes he causes the skin to be torn off their foreheads, and on the naked bones to be stamped with a red hot iron the marks of ignominy. Again, he causes others to be cloven through in the form of a cross; or to be compressed with ropes until they are entirely deformed; or to be beaten with ox's sinews until they are rendered unrecognizable. [See Gretzer, De Cruce, lib. iv. c. 32, pp. 628-629.]

A great lesson! Let this hatred of satan for the Sign of the Cross be the measure of our love for the adorable sign, and our confidence in it. You shall see to-morrow, that it has other claims on these two sentiments.

Mgr. J.J. Gaume

Eleventh Letter

The Sign of the Cross is a treasure that enriches us, because it is a prayer: proofs — A powerful prayer: proofs — A universal prayer: proofs — It supplies all our wants — For his soul man needs lights — The Sign of the Cross obtains them: proofs — Examples of the Martyrs

December 6th

My Dear Frederic,

The Sign of the Cross is a treasure which enriches us; this is one of the reasons of its being. It enriches us, because it is an excellent prayer. This is, my dear friend, as you have not forgotten, the point of doctrine we have just established.

Half the proof has already been given. It is in the antiquity, the universality, the perpetuity of the Sign of the Cross. In the midst of the shipwreck in which the idolatrous world allowed so many primitive revelations to be lost or damaged, we see the Sign of the Cross floating on the surface. What says this strange fact, new to you, incomprehensible to a great number, but most reasonable to the Christian accustomed to reflect? It speaks eloquently of the high utility of the Sign of the Cross for man, because it tells its powerful efficacy over the heart of God. From reasoning, let us proceed to facts.

The Sign of the Cross is a prayer; a powerful, universal prayer.

It is a prayer. What is a man who prays? He is one who confesses his indigence before God; his intellectual, moral, and material indigence. He is a beggar at the rich man's door. Now, the beggar prays with his voice, but more eloquently by his pale and emaciated face, by his infirmities, his tattered clothes and his attitude. Thus prayed on the Cross the adorable Mendicant of Calvary. In that state, the Son of God was more than ever the object of the infinite complacency of His Father. He Himself tells us that that eloquent prayer, more in action than in words, was the powerful lever which drew all things to Him. [St. John, 12:33.]

What does a man do when he forms the Sign of the Cross, either with his hand, or by extending his arms? He impresses upon himself the image of the Divine Mendicant; he identifies himself with him. It is Jacob clothing himself with the garments of Esau, that he may obtain the paternal benediction. What does he say to God? By this attitude of faith, humility, and devotedness, he says: "Behold in me your Christ, *respice in faciem Christi tui* (look on the face of thy Christ);" a prayer more eloquent than all the words that could be spoken. "It ascends," says St. Ambrose, "and the alms descend." *Ascendit deprecatio et descendit Dei miseratio.*

Such is the Sign of the Cross, even without a formula. It does not speak, yet it says all. It is a powerful prayer. When an agent of the authorities, a commissary of police, mayor, or gendarme, lays his hand upon a culprit, he says: "I arrest you in the name of the law." In the words, "In the name of the law," the guilty man sees the authority of his country, the strength of the army, the judges, the king himself; and he allows himself to be taken.

When, then, man, threatened by danger, assailed by doubts, persecuted by temptation, a prey to suffering and sickness, pronounces these words of solemn authority, "In the name of the Father, and of the Son, and of the Holy Ghost," and while pronouncing them makes the sign by which the world has been redeemed, and hell vanquished, how can you explain the continued resistance of evil? Has not man fulfilled all the conditions of success? Is not God, in some way, obliged to intervene, and by His intervention, to glorify His Name and the power of Christ?

The particular efficacy of the Sign of the Cross has never been doubted, either by the Church, or by Christian generations. The gravest theologians teach even that the Sign of the Cross operates of itself, and independently of him who makes it. They give us several proofs: I will cite only two.

The first, is the custom of incessantly repeating the Sign of the Cross. "If it did not produce," say they, "its effects of itself, Christians would have no reason for making use of it so frequently. What good would it do to have recourse to it, when a motion of the soul, or any good action whatsoever, would suffice to obtain or realize what they hope to obtain or realize by the Sign of the Cross." [Gretzer, lib. iv. c. 62, p. 703. Gregorius de Valentia, Suarez, Bellarminus, Pyræus, et al.]

The second rests on facts celebrated in history, and of incontestable authenticity: I will relate a few.

The first, is that of Julian the Apostate. A deserter from the true God, that emperor, becomes, by an inevitable conclusion, an adorer of the demon. To learn the secrets of the future, he seeks throughout Greece for men in communication with the Evil Spirit. A sorcerer presents himself, who promises to satisfy his curiosity. Julian is conducted into a temple of the idols. The conjurations are pronounced, and the emperor sees himself surrounded by demons, whose appearance fills him with terror.

By a gesture of thoughtless fear, he makes the Sign of the Cross, and the demons disappear. The sorcerer complains, and repeats his incantations. The demons reappear. Julian forgets himself again, and at the Sign of the Cross, the spirits of darkness again take flight. [Orat. I., contr. Julian.]

This fact, related by St. Gregory Nazianzen, Theodoret, and other Fathers of the Church, caused great excitement in the East.

The second, is better known in the West. We have it from Pope St. Gregory. The illustrious pontiff commences his relation by the following words. "The fact which I am about to relate, is not doubtful, for it had almost as many witnesses as the town of Fondi numbered inhabitants. [Dial., lib. iii. c. 7.]

"A Jew, journeying from Campania to Rome by the Appian Way, arrived at the small town of Fondi. It being very late, he could find no lodging, and went to pass the night in an old temple of Apollo. He felt afraid of that ancient dwelling of the demons, and although not a Christian, took care to arm himself with the Sign of the Cross.

"Frightened at his solitude, he remained awake until midnight. Suddenly he saw a troop of demons, who seemed to be coming to pay homage to their chief, who was seated at the head of the temple. As they presented themselves, he interrogated each in particular as to what he had done to lead men into sin. All revealed to him their artifices. In the midst of the discourse one advanced, who related that he had succeeded in making the venerable bishop of the city feel the sting of a terrible temptation.

" 'Until now,' said he, 'my labor was in vain, but last evening I succeeded in making him give a slight tap on the shoulder of the holy woman employed in his house.'

" 'Continue,' answered the ancient enemy of mankind, 'continue and finish what you have begun, and so great a victory shall bring you an extraordinary reward.'

"Meanwhile, the Jew, the witness of the spectacle, could scarcely breathe. In order to make him die of fear, the president of the infernal assembly, knowing of his presence, ordered them to inform him who was that rash man who had dared to take shelter in the temple. The evil spirits approached, but seeing him marked with the Sign of the Cross, cried out: 'Væ, væ! vas vacuum et signatum! (Woe! woe! an empty vessel, sealed)!' At those words, the infernal troop disappeared.

"The Jew, on his side, hastened to depart. He hurried to the church, where he found the venerable bishop. Calling him aside, he related all that had happened to him, and how he had learned of the slight tap given to his servant, and what was the project of the demon. Surprised beyond measure, the bishop immediately dismissed her, and from that time forbade all persons of the other sex to enter his house. He consecrated the old temple of Apollo in honor of St. Andrew, and the Jew was converted." [Dial., lib. iii. ch. 7.]

Let us relate another fact. We read in the Ecclesiastical History of Nicephorus, that under the emperor Mauritius, Chosroes II., king of Persia, sent an embassy to Constantinople, and that all the Persians who composed it had the Sign of the Cross marked on their foreheads.

The emperor asked them why it was that they bore a sign in which they did not believe.

"What you see on our foreheads," said they, "is the testimony of a signal favor which we received some time ago. A pestilence was ravaging our country, and some Christians advised us to mark the Sign of the Cross on our foreheads, as a preservative against it. We believed them, and have been saved, although nearly all our families were cut off by the scourge. [Hist., lib. xviii. c. 20.]

After these facts naturally follows the reflection of the great

Bishop of Hippo, which seems decisive in favor of the teachings of theologians. "We must not be surprised," says he, "at the power of the Sign of the Cross when it is made by good Christians, since it has so much strength when employed by strangers, who do not believe in it, and this happens for the glory of the great King." [Lib. de 83 quæst., quæst. 79.]

That we may remain within the limits of orthodoxy, we must, however, add that the Sign of the Cross does not operate of itself, purely and simply, but in as much as is useful for our salvation and that of others. It is the same with it as with certain other practices, such as, for example, exorcisms, to which no divine promise attaches effects infallible and unconditional.

I add, that the piety of him who makes the Sign of the Cross contributes to its efficacy. This sign is a silent invocation of Jesus Crucified; consequently, it is so much the more efficacious, as it is made with greater fervor. Again, the invocation with the heart or the mouth is so much the more likely to obtain its effect, as the Christian who makes it is more virtuous and more agreeable to the Lord. [Gretzer, ubi supra.]

It is a universal prayer. In one sense the Sign of the Cross may say, like Our Saviour Himself: "All power has been given to me in heaven and on earth." Here, more than anywhere else, we must, my dear Frederic, reason with facts. They are so numerous that the only difficulty is to choose among them. All, and each in its manner, proclaim on one side the faith of our ancestors, and on the other, the empire of the Sign of the Cross over the visible and invisible worlds. It provides for all the wants of both soul and body.

For his soul, man has need of lights; the Sign of the Cross obtains them. St. Porphyrus, Bishop of Gaza, is obliged to dispute with a Manichean woman. In order to dispel, by the clearness of his reasoning, the darkness with which the unfortunate woman is surrounded, he makes the Sign of the Cross, and light shines on that darkened intellect.

Julian, the crowned sophist, provokes a controversy with Cæsarius, brother of St. Gregory Nazianzen. The generous athlete enters the lists armed with the Sign of the Cross. To an enemy perfect in that art of warfare, and skilful in his manner of reasoning, he opposes the standard of the Word, and the spirit of lies is caught in his own snares. [S. Greg. Nazian. In laud Cæsar.]

St. Cyril of Jerusalem, so powerful in words and deeds, orders recourse to be had to the Sign of the Cross every time that he is to engage in combat with the pagans, and he assures them that they shall be reduced to silence. [Catech., xiii.] In the temporal order, no less than in the spiritual, divine lights are necessary to man; they also are obtained by the Sign of the Cross. The emperors of the East, the successors of Constantine, when they had to speak before the Senate, always began by the Sign of the Cross. [Coripp. Deland. Justin. jun.]

As we have already seen, St. Louis, before discussing in council the affairs of his kingdom, always conformed himself to this most ancient and religious practice.

If, after the example of the greatest princes who have governed the world, the emperors and kings of the nineteenth century should have recourse to the Sign of the Cross, do you think that affairs should be in a worse state than they are? As for me, I am as convinced as I am of my own existence, that they would be much better.

Are not those who govern now, as much in need of light as those who governed in former times? Do they pretend to find it elsewhere than in Him who is its source? Do they know of a means more certain to invoke Him with success? Do not all ages bear witness to its efficacy? Does not the Church, which ought to be their oracle, continue to proclaim it? Is there a council, a conclave, or a religious assembly that is not begun with the Sign of the Cross? Do the Catholics priests, faithful inheritors of tradition, ever speak from the pulpit without being armed with this sign of strength and light? In this they observe the precept of the ancient Fathers.

"*Fac hoc signum et loqueris;* (make the Sign of the Cross, and you shall speak)," says St. Cyril of Jerusalem. [Catech. illuminat., iv.]

What I have said of kings, my dear friend, must be said of all those who are charged with teaching others.

Is not the Incarnate Word the God of science and of all sciences, the Professor of professors, the Master of masters?

If the Sign of the Cross presided over all the lessons that are now given, over all the books that are now printed, do you think we would be inundated, as we are, with errors, sophistry, false ideas, and incoherent systems, whose incontestable result is to cause the modern world to sink again into that intellectual darkness from which Christianity has drawn it?

For his soul, man needs strength: the Sign of the Cross is the fruitful source of it. Look at your illustrious ancestors, the martyrs. From what did they seek the courage to triumph in their heroic combats? From the Sign of the Cross. Generals of armies, centurions, soldiers, magistrates, senators, patricians, and plebeians, children and aged men, matrons and young virgins, all were careful, when descending into the arena, to cover themselves with this invincible armor: *insuperabili christianorum armatura.*

Come with me; I will name a few to you. In Cæsarea, see that generous martyr, who walks to the place of execution surrounded by an immense concourse of people. It is the centurion Gordius. See him, calm and collected, arming his forehead with the Sign of the Cross. [S. Basil, Orat. in S. Gord.] What is that town in Armenia, situated in the midst of snows, and on the borders of a frozen lake? It is Sebaste. Behold, coming here in the evening, forty men, bound with cords, and stripped of their garments, who are being dragged to the midst of the lake, condemned to pass the night there. Who are they? Forty veterans of the army of Licinius. A superhuman force of resistance is so much the more necessary, because on the shore, warm baths are prepared for those who will apostatize. They make the Sign of the Cross, and an heroic death comes to crown their courage. [Encom. in 40 SS. Martyr.]

We have seen the young Agnes as a living Sign of the Cross amidst the flames. Behold other Christian virgins, born like her in the Golden Age of the martyrs. The first is St. Thecla, illustrious by her birth, more illustrious by her faith. The executioners have seized upon her; they conduct her to the funeral pile; she mounts it with a firm step, makes the Sign of the Cross, and remains calm and tranquil in the midst of the flames. At the same moment, the rain descends in torrents, the flames are extinguished; and, like the children of Babylon, the young heroine comes forth from the fire without one hair of her head being injured. [Ado, in Martyrol., Sept. 23.]

The second is St. Euphemia, no less celebrated than the first. Upon the orders of the judge, the instruments of torture are made ready in an instant. The young virgin is about to be stretched on the wheel: she makes the Sign of the Cross, and advances toward the frightful engine, bristling with iron spikes; she gazes on it without any terror, and by that glance, causes it to fly into fragments. [Apud. Sur. t. v. et Baron. Martyrol., Sept. 16.]

Look again. We stand in one of the Roman prætoriums, so often crimsoned with the blood of our fathers, so often the witnesses of their sublime answers and their heroic constancy. It is during the persecutions of Decius; you know that sanguinary emperor, as Lactantius calls him: *execrabile animal Decius* (that execrable animal Decius). Before the judge stands a band of Christians. The accuser comes, according to custom, to charge them with all sorts of crimes. They are already condemned; they know it. What do they do? Raising their eyes to heaven they make the Sign of the Cross, and say to the proconsul, "You shall see that we are neither cowardly nor faint-hearted." [Apud. sur. Apr. 13.] Were I to continue this list, I should have to cause the innumerable army of martyrs to pass before you in review.

There is not one of those valorous soldiers of the Crucified, who, in going to combat, did not bear the standard of his King. Let it suffice to name a few. St. Julian and St. Pontian, St. Constant and St. Crescent, St. Isidore, St. Nazarius and St. Celsus, St. Maximinus, St. Alexander, St. Sophia and her three daughters, St. Paul and St. Juliana, St. Cyprian and St. Justina. [See their Acts]

Taken from all countries and all conditions, they bear witness that it was a universal custom among the martyrs to arm themselves with that sign of strength, before entering the lists with men, with beasts, or with the elements.

But better still; fearing that the weight of the chains would prevent them from forming the Sign of the Cross, they ask the Christians, their brethren, or the priests, their fathers, to arm them with the victorious sign. Corribonus, converted to the faith by the martyr St. Eleutherius, goes himself into the amphitheatre to seek the crown of martyrdom.

"Pray for me," says he to his father in Jesus Christ, "and arm me with the Sign of the Cross, the same with which you have armed Felix the general." [Apud. sur., Apr. 18.]

Glyceria, the noble daughter of a father thrice consul, is seized and cast into a narrow prison. The first act she performs on seeing herself in the hands of her enemies, is to beg the holy priest, Philocratus, to make the Sign of the Cross on her forehead. The priest grants her desire, saying, "May this sign of the Crucified fulfill all your desires." [Ibid., t. iii. et Baron. t. ii.] They are all accomplished.

The young heroine descends into the amphitheatre. At the moment she is about to gather the palm of victory, she turns toward the Christians, who mingle with the crowd, and says with all the spirit of a warrior about to die for his flag: "Brethren, sisters, children, fathers, and all you who hold to me the place of a mother, beware; watch over yourselves, and consider well who is the Emperor whose mark and sign is engraved on our foreheads." [Ibid.]

You have heard it; in the Sign of the Cross all the martyrs sought for strength. And would they have looked for strength from a nonentity? Would the great Emperor for whom they died, have allowed them to remain in an incurable illusion? If any one believes this, let him give his proofs.

I shall write soon again.

Mgr. J.J. Gaume

Twelfth Letter

Perpetual necessity of the Sign of the Cross to obtain strength—Its recommendations and practice by the chiefs of the spiritual combat—The Sign of the Cross in temptations—The Sign of the Cross at death—Examples of the martyrs—Examples of true Christians dying a natural death—The dying caused the Sign of the Cross to be made on them by their brethren

December 7th

Dear Frederic,

The Sign of the Cross has lost nothing of its power or necessity. It is true, that the tyrants are dead, and the amphitheatres in ruins. The Sign of the Cross has vanquished the one and overthrown the other. If the second are not rebuilt, the first, from time to time, arise from their graves. The race of Neros shall never be extinct; the most formidable is yet to come. With ancient fury, those who have appeared since the Cæsars have decimated the Christians; that other race equally immortal, *expeditum morti genus* (that race devoted to death), as Tertullian says. What they did yesterday in the West, they do to-day in the East; they will do again to-morrow wherever they shall reign.

Advice to combatants:—let no one forget where is the source of strength. Until that time, remember, dear friend, *habet et pax martyres suos*, (that peace has also her martyrs). Who is the man who does not carry within himself one or more Neros? Is there one day of his rational life, or even hour, in which he has not to watch and to fight? What do I say? Twenty times a day, seducing objects present themselves before him, evil thoughts importune his mind, rebellious senses solicit his heart to commit the basest treasons. Oh! how greatly is he in need of strength!

Where shall he find it? In the Sign of the Cross. The testimony of ages, the experience of both veterans and young soldiers, attest to-day, as they did yesterday, the sovereign power of the Sign of the Cross to dissipate seductive charms, expel evil thoughts, and repress the motions of concupiscence.

Listen to Prudentius, the poet of the martyrs, who knew both the details of their triumphs and the secret of their victories. "*Fac cum vocante somno Castum petis cubile, Frontem locumque cordis Crucis figura signet: Crux pellet omne crimen, Fugiunt crucem tenebræ. Tali dicata signo Mens fluctuare nescit.* (When, at the call of sleep, you go to your chaste bed, make the Sign of the Cross on your forehead and heart. The Cross shall preserve you from all sin; before it shall fly the powers of darkness; the soul sanctified by this sign, cannot waver.)" [Apud. S. Greg. Turon., lib. I. Miraculi., c. 106.]

Hear also those generals of the eternal combat, those great geniuses and great saints, consummate in the art of spiritual warfare, which is called asceticism; they all, with one voice, recommend Christian soldiers to make use of the Sign of the Cross.

"Do you feel your heart inflamed?" says St. Chrysostom. "Make the Sign of the Cross on your breast, and your anger shall be dissipated like smoke." [In Math. Hom. 88.]

And St. Augustine:—"Does Amalec, your enemy, try to bar the way and hinder you from advancing? Make the Sign of the Cross, and he shall be vanquished." [Lib. 50. *Homil.*, Homil. 20.]

And Mark, the great servant of God, who foretold to the Emperor Leo the hour of his death:—"I have learned by my own experience, that the Sign of the Cross appeases interior troubles, and procures the health of the soul. As soon as the Sign of the Cross is made, grace operates; all is appeased, the flesh as well as the heart." [Biblioth. pp. t. v.]

St. Maximus of Turin:—"It is from the Sign of the Cross we must expect the cure of all our wounds. If the venom of avarice be diffused through our veins, let us make the Sign of the Cross, and the venom shall be expelled.

"If the scorpion of voluptuousness sting us, let us have recourse to the same means, and we shall be healed.

"If grossly terrestrial thoughts seek to defile us, let us again have recourse to the Sign of the Cross, and we shall live the divine life." [Apud. S. Ambr. serm. 55.]

St. Bernard:—"Who is the man so completely master of his thoughts as never to have impure ones? But it is necessary to repress their attacks immediately, that we may vanquish the enemy there where he hoped to triumph. The infallible means of success is to make the Sign of the Cross." [De passion. Dom. c. xix. n. 65.]

St. Peter Damian:—"If you feel a bad thought arise in your mind, immediately make the Sign of the Cross with your thumb, and be assured that it shall be dissipated." [Instit. Monast.]

The pious Ecberth:—"Nothing is more efficacious than the Sign of the Cross to dissipate temptations, even the most shameful." [Lib. viar. Domin., c. xxi.]

To sum up all those testimonies:—"Whatever may be the temptations that oppress us," concludes St. Gregory of Tours, "we must repulse them. For this end, we should make, not carelessly, but courageously, the Sign of the Cross, either on our forehead or our breast." [Ubi supra.]

If it were necessary, one thousand facts could be given to confirm what you have just heard. One will suffice. It is a revelation with which a fervent religious, named Patroclus, was favored, and by which God showed him the sovereign power of the Sign of the Cross against temptation.

One day, the demon, transforming himself into an angel of light, appeared to the venerable abbot. He tried to persuade him, with artful words, to abandon his solitude and return to the world. But the man of God feeling a pestilential fire coursing through his veins, prostrated himself in prayer, and begged God to make him accomplish His holy will. His prayer was heard. An angel appeared to him and said: "If you desire to know the world, ascend this column, and see what it is."

Being ravished into an ecstasy, the pious solitary believed he saw before him a column of prodigious height. He ascended it, and beheld homicides, thefts, massacres, fornications, and all the enormous crimes of the universe. "Alas!" exclaimed he, as he descended, "alas, my Lord, do not permit that I should return to the midst of so many abominations."

The angel answered: "Cease then to regret the world, lest you perish with it. Go rather into your oratory, to pray the Lord that you may find support in the midst of the trials of your pilgrimage." He obeyed, and there found the Sign of the Cross engraved on a brick. He understood the gift of God, and knew that that sign was an impregnable fortress against temptation. [St. Gregory of Tours, Vit. Part., c. 9.]

A martyr of war, or a martyr of peace; such is a man during his life. What is he in death? Look at that sick man, a prey to pain, abandoned by everybody, or surrounded by parents and friends who are utterly powerless. Behind him, time, which flies; before him, eternity, which advances, and into which he finds himself passing, without any human power being able to retard the moment of his departure, or mitigate the anguish of the journey. That sick man is you, my dear friend; it is I, it is every man, rich or poor, subject or monarch. If, during the warfare of life, we stand in need of light, strength, consolation, and hope; tell me, is not our need a thousand times greater in the decisive struggle of death? Well! the Sign of the Cross supplies all. Under this new point of view, how dear it was to our ancestors, and how dear ought it to be to us!

As the martyrs, when going to their last combat, failed not to fortify themselves with the Sign of the Cross, so the true Christians of every age have had incessant recourse to the same sign, to alleviate their sufferings and sanctify their deaths. I will cite a few examples.

Speaking of his beloved sister, St. Macrina, whom he himself assisted in her last moments, St. Gregory of Nyssa, writes as follows: " 'Lord,' said she, 'in order to put the enemy to flight, and to protect the lives of those who fear Thee, Thou hast given them the Sign of the Cross.' In pronouncing these words, she formed the adorable sign on her eyes, her lips, and her heart. [Vit. S. Macr.]

His illustrious brother, St. Gregory Nazianzen, defying the demon, said to him: "If you dare to attack me at the moment of my death, beware: for I shall put you shamefully to flight by the Sign of the Cross." [Carm. 22.]

Instead of making it with the hand, the early Christians very frequently, when dying, extended their arms. This is what they called "*sacrificium vespertinum,* (the evening sacrifice)." To this manner of making the Sign of the Cross, Arnobius applies the words of the Psalmist, "The lifting up of my hands is my evening sacrifice," and says: "May such be our evening sacrifice, I mean that of the evening of our lives, when we are really about to offer the evening sacrifice; and may our attention be directed to raise our hands in the form of a Cross, that we may rejoice in the Saviour Jesus, at the moment that we go to Him." [In Ps. 140.]

It was in the like attitude that St. Paul, the patriarch of the desert, died, and in which he was found by St. Anthony. [S. Hier., De Vit. S. Paul.]

The same spectacle was presented by St. Pachomius. "Being at the point of death," says the author of his life, "he armed himself with the Sign of the Cross; beheld with great joy the angel of the Lord approaching him, and gave up his holy soul to God." [Life of St. Pachomius, c. 53.]

In the same manner died St. Ambrose.

"On the last day of his life," writes the priest Paulinus, "from about the eleventh hour until he gave up his holy soul to God, he prayed with his arms extended in the form of a Cross." [Paulin. in Vit. S. Ambr.]

From Milan let us proceed to Constantinople. Behold another bishop at the point of death. "St. Eutychius," says his historian, "was seized with a violent fever towards the middle of the night. He remained in that state for seven days, never ceasing to pray and to fortify himself with the Sign of the Cross." [Apud. sur. Jul. 2.]

Let us end our journey by passing through France; let us assist at the deaths of some of her kings. Let us stop for a moment at Aix-la-chapelle, and behold the last moments of the great emperor. "The next day being come," says a bishop, an eye-witness, "Charlemagne, knowing what he ought to do, extended his right hand, and as well as he could made the Sign of the Cross on his forehead, his breast, and every part of his body." [Thegan. De gestis Ludov. Imper.] Thus did that great man before his death.

Look at his son, Louis the Pious. "Having arranged all his

affairs, and made his last requests, he ordered that the evening office should be recited near him, and a relic of the True Cross be placed upon his breast. During that time he himself, as much as his strength allowed, made the Sign of the Cross on his forehead and his heart. When he became too weak, he begged his brother to continue to do it for him. [Apud. Gretzer.]

Let us come to one of his successors, the most worthy of the throne, the good King Robert. During the last days of his life, he never ceased, both by voice and gesture, to call the saints of heaven to his aid, and continually fortified himself by making the Sign of the Cross on his forehead, eyes, nostrils, lips, throat, and ears, in memory of the Incarnation of Our Lord, of His Nativity, Passion, Resurrection and Ascension, and of the Holy Ghost. Such had been, during his life, the custom of this prince, who was never wilfully without having holy water with him. [Helgald., in Epitom. Vit. Robert.]

Let us cite another, Louis le Gros. Seeing himself near death, he caused a carpet to be laid on the ground, and ashes to be spread over it in the form of a Cross. Being laid by his officers upon that bed, which reminded him of that of the King of Calvary, the virtuous monarch continued to make the Sign of the Cross even to his last breath. [Gretzer, p. 617.]

For a king to die like a God; is there anything degrading in this? What degrades a man, is to die without understanding death, to die with the insensibility of a beast.

You have seen that the martyrs, fearing that when dying they should not be able to make the Sign of the Cross themselves, begged their Christian brethren to make it for them. The same was done by our ancestors who died a natural death.

Besides the example of Louis le Débonnaire, of whom you

have just read, I will remind you of a few others. Taken from the first ages, they will show the perpetuity of the tradition.

St. Zenobius, the intimate friend of St. Ambrose, being on the point of terminating his beautiful life by a precious death, raised his hand and made the Sign of the Cross on every person around him. Then he begged the bishops to make on him with their consecrated hands, the sign of the strength, hope, and salvation. [Apud. sur. May 25.]

From the death-bed of a priest let us pass to that of one of the faithful. Behold here a devoted daughter, who assists her tender, her illustrious mother. In our day the greater number content themselves with bestowing on their dearest friends only material cares. They would reproach themselves, were they to omit the least prescription of the physician. But what of Christian assistance? What of the prescription of the Divine Physician, and of our Mother, the Church? With what care do they attend to those? To the most devoted bodily care, our ancestors, far wiser and better than we, added the remedies of the soul.

Then in Bethlehem, the illustrious daughter of Fabius, St. Paula, lies at the point of death. By her bedside is Eustochium, worthy daughter of her mother. How is that angel of tenderness occupied?

"She never ceased," says St. Jerome, "to form the Sign of the Cross on the lips and breast of her mother, endeavoring to alleviate her sufferings by the impression of that consoling sign." [In Epitaph Paulæ.]

You see then, that both in life and death, the Sign of the Cross was constantly employed by our ancestors to obtain for themselves and others, light, strength, resignation, courage, and hope. "*Magna res signum crucis* (What a great thing, then, is the Sign of the Cross)!" cries out, with good reason, one who was witness to its admirable effects. [S. Elig. De rectitud. Catech., etc., inter op. S. Aug. t. vi.]

To-morrow we shall see its efficacy in a new order of things.

Mgr. J.J. Gaume

Thirteenth Letter

Effects of the Sign of the Cross in the temporal order—It cures all diseases, and removes whatever can harm us—It gives sight to the blind, hearing to the deaf, speech to the dumb, the use of their limbs to the lame and paralyzed; cures other maladies, and restores life to the dead

December 8th

My Dear Frederic,

Poor and indigent in the spiritual order, man is not less so in the temporal; his body and soul subsist only by alms.

Among the good things necessary for the body, there are two in particular, my dear friend, which I will point out to you; health and security. The Sign of the Cross is efficacious to procure both one and the other.

Health. The Incarnate Word is the living and vivifying life. Speaking of Him when He dwelt among men, the Gospel tells us in words as simple as sublime, "*virtus de illo exibat et sanabat omnes;* (virtue went out from Him and healed all)." [St. Luke VI, 19]

History teaches us that these words may be applied in their full extent to the Sign of the Cross. Nothing is more fully established than that this sign was used by the first Christians to heal the sick. St. Cyril, and St. John Chrysostom, the one patriarch of Jerusalem, the other of Constantinople, assure us positively, that the Sign of the Cross continued in their time, as well as in that of their ancestors, to cure the sick, and heal the bites of ferocious beasts. [Catech., xiii; S. Chrys. In Math., hom. 54.]

Let us come to proofs. All man's senses are subject to disease; let us begin with the most noble, the sight. If, instead of continually poring over pagan authors, our young students had sometimes read the acts of the martyrs, they would have seen in those of St. Laurence the striking miracle of which the Church sings even to this day, *qui per signum crucis cæcos illuminavit* (who through the sign of the cross gives sight to the blind).

The illustrious archdeacon of Rome had entered the house of a Christian, in which was a blind man named Crescentius, who, melting into tears, threw himself at the feet of the saint, saying: "Place your hand over my eyes, that I may see you." The blessed Laurence, deeply affected, said: "May Our Lord Jesus Christ, who opened the eyes of the man born blind, give you light." At the same time he made the Sign of the Cross on the eyes of Crescentius, who saw the light and the blessed Laurence, as he had desired." [Apud sur., Aug. 10.]

The learned Theodoret relates of his own mother what follows: "My mother had a sore eye, which baffled all the resources of medicine. We had turned over the leaves of every volume, and examined all the old authors, but none gave the remedy applicable to the present evil. We were all there, when a friend of my mother's called to see her. She told her of a man of God, named Peter, and related a miracle which had been operated by him. 'The wife of the Governor of the East,' said she, 'had the same disease as you. She addressed herself to Peter, who is from Pergamus, and he cured her by praying for her and making on her the Sign of the Cross.'

"My mother lost not one instant. She went to find the man of God, threw herself at his feet, and conjured him to heal her. He answered, 'I am but a poor sinner, and am far from possessing that power with God which you suppose me to have.' My mother redoubled her entreaties and tears, protesting that she would not leave him until he had cured her.

" 'God,' said he to her, 'is the Physician for those evils. [The saint reasoned like Ambrose Paré, the father of French surgery: "I dress it, and God cures it."] He always hears the prayers of those that believe. He will hear you, not in view of my merits, but because of your faith. If then, yours is sincere, true, pure, and without doubt, laying aside medicine and physicians, accept the remedy that God gives you.' At those words he stretched his hand over her eye, made the Sign of the Cross, and the disease was healed." [Hist. S. S. Pater. in Petro.]

Facts nearer our time will show you that in traversing centuries, the Sign of the Cross has never ceased to be the best oculist. St. Eligius, Bishop of Noyon, in crossing one of the bridges in Paris, cured a blind man, who, instead of asking for alms, begged him to make the Sign of the Cross on his eyes. [Life of the Saint, by S. Owen, Bp. Of Rouen, c. xxix.]

A miracle very like this is seen in the life of St. Frobert, abbot of a monastery near Troyes in Champagne. He was yet only a child, when his mother, who had been blind for many years, took him on her knee; then embracing and caressing him, she asked him to make the Sign of the Cross on her eyes. The young saint at first refused, but at length overcome by her maternal entreaties, invoked the name of the Lord, made the Sign of the Cross as required, and at that instant his mother recovered her sight. [His Life, Dec. 31st.]

In the life of St. Bernard, Mabillon cites more than thirty blind persons of every age and condition, in France, Germany, and Italy, cured in the presence of kings and great nobles, by means of the Sign of the Cross, made over them by the Thaumaturgus of Clairvaux. [T. II.]

From the sight, let us pass to the hearing. Like Our Lord Himself, the Sign of the Cross makes the deaf to hear, and the dumb to speak.

Behold us in the midst of the great city of Rome, in the palace of the prefect. Before us stands a young and brilliant officer; he is called Sebastian. This name, illustrious among all others, is never heard in our colleges. You must know, then, that St. Sebastian was commandant of the first prætorian cohort, under Diocletian. In our modern language we would say, colonel of a regiment of the Imperial Guard.

Endowed with eloquence equal to his intrepidity, he employed the gifts of God to encourage the martyrs who were brought daily to the prætorium. One day Zoë, the wife of the prefect of Rome, who had been dumb for six years, had the happiness of assisting at his discourse. Although a pagan, she was so much moved that she cast herself at the feet of the saint, and tried to make him understand by gestures that she desired to be cured.

She was understood. The Sign of the Cross made on her mouth instantly restored her speech, and the first use she made of it was to ask for baptism. [Act. de S. Sebast.]

Tell them, also, that by the same sign the immortal Abbot of Clairvaux, St. Bernard cured a number of deaf and dumb persons. At Cologne, a girl deaf for many years; at Bourlémont, a child deaf and dumb from her birth; at Bale, a deaf man; at Metz, a deaf person in presence of an immense concourse of people; at Constance, at Spire, at Maestricht, persons both deaf and dumb; at Troyes, a lame and dumb girl in presence of the bishops, Geoffrey of Langres and Henry of Troyes. In fine, at Clairvaux, a deaf and dumb child, who had been awaiting his arrival for fifteen days. [Mabillon, *ubi supra*.]

While the saint was at Spire, where he wrought many miraculous cures, Anselm, bishop of Havelberg, arrived there. He had a very sore throat, and was scarcely able either to speak or swallow.

"You ought to cure me also," said he to St. Bernard.

"If you had as much faith as these good women," answered the Abbot of Clairvaux, pleasantly, "I could, perhaps, render you the same service."

"If my faith is not sufficient," answered the bishop, "let yours cure me."

The saint touched him, making the Sign of the Cross, and the pain and swelling disappeared at the same instant. [Vit. lib. vi. c. 5. n. 19.]

Diffused throughout the whole body, the sense of touch is that which presents a greater surface to the attacks of disease. How can we detail the evils, more or less painful, to which it is exposed?

But numerous as they are, it is consoling to know that none can elude the salutary power of the Sign of the Cross. By its virtue we recognize Him who healed *omnem languorem in populo*; (all kinds of maladies among the people.)

St. Germanus, one of the most holy and amiable bishops that have governed the diocese of Paris, was one day going to visit St. Hilary of Poitiers, his worthy colleague. As he was on his way, two men brought to him with great difficulty a poor woman both lame and dumb. The saint had no sooner made the Sign of the Cross on her, than she recovered her speech and the use of her limbs. Three days afterwards, she went to return thanks to her benefactor. [Vita, c. xlvi.]

A like miracle was wrought by St. Euthymius, the great archimandrite of Palestine. Terebon, son of the governor of the Saracens, in Arabia, had been from his early youth paralyzed in one half of his body. Having heard the holy abbot spoken of, he begged to be conducted to him; his request was granted, and his father and a great number of the barbarians accompanied him. The saint made the Sign of the Cross on Terebon, who was immediately cured. This cure was followed by the conversion, not only of the father and son, but also of the Saracens, the companions of their journey and witnesses of the miracle.

Long afterwards, St. Vincent Ferrer operated in France the same prodigy as that which had rejoiced the East. As he was at Nantes, they brought him a man who had been paralyzed for eighteen years, and asked him to give him his blessing. "I have neither gold nor silver," said the saint to the sick man, "but I pray Our Lord to give you health of body and soul." Then he made the Sign of the Cross over his limbs. At the same moment the paralytic, entirely cured, rose up and gave thanks to God and the saint; then he returned home, and never again felt his former disease. [Fleury. Hist. eccl. lib. xxiv, n. 28.]

Such is, sometimes, the violence of pain, that it occasions delirium, and thus deprives the unfortunate son of Adam of the health both of body and soul. The Sign of the Cross forces the malady from this new entrenchment.

Edmer, the historian of St. Anselm, Archbishop of Canterbury, relates that the holy man in going to Cluny, cured, by means of the Sign of the Cross, a woman who had lost her mind, and become furious. [Vit. S. Anselm, lib. ii.]

St. Bernard did the same at Sechingen and Cologne. In the latter city, they presented to him a woman who had become a maniac, on account of the death of her husband and child. The unfortunate woman employed all her strength against herself, so that they were obliged to keep her in chains. The saint, moved with compassion, made the Sign of the Cross over her, by which she was immediately restored to her reason and full possession of her faculties. [Mabillon, *ubi supra,* lib. iv. c. 6. n. 33.]

The Word, the Redeemer, whom the Gospel so often shows to us curing the most obstinate fevers, has communicated to the Sign of the Cross the virtue of operating the like prodigies.

St. Prixus, bishop of Clermont in Auvergne, having arrived at the monastery of Darouge in the Vosges, found the abbot Amarinus ill with so malignant a fever that he was unable to walk or to swallow anything, except a few drops of water. The holy bishop had recourse to his ordinary weapons, and paid for his welcome by a miracle. He made the Sign of the Cross on the sick man, who rose up, perfectly cured. [Life of SS., Jan. 26th.]

It has the same power with regard to epilepsy, a malady much more difficult to be healed. In the life of St. Malachy, Archbishop of Armagh, who died at Clairvaux, St. Bernard says: "Before starting for Rome, whither he was going to receive the pallium from the hands of Pope Eugenius III., the holy archbishop restored health to an epileptic by making the Sign of the Cross on the breast of the unfortunate man, who used to fall down many times in a day.

St. Bernard himself wrought a similar miracle in favor of a girl from Troyes, in Champagne. Such had been the malignity of the disease, that she had lost the power of speech. The holy abbot imposed hands and made the Sign of the Cross over her; at the same moment, being restored to complete health, she spoke to those present. [Mabillon, *ubi supra,* c. xiv. n. 47.]

Our Lord has said, "After my example, heal the lepers." His disciples have received this command, and its divine virtue has passed into the Sign of the Cross. St. Francis Xavier filled the East with the renown of his name. His fame reached the ears of a leper who during many years had sought in vain for his cure.

Not daring to appear in public, he conjured the saint to visit him.

Xavier, being much occupied, could not yield to the desires of the poor man, but sent one of his companions to ask him if he would believe in the Gospel, in case he should be healed. If he promised to embrace the faith, the deputy was to make the Sign of the Cross over him three times. All was done as Xavier had ordered. Scarcely had the leper given the promise, when his body became as clean as if he had never been infected with the leprosy. [Life, lib. v. p. 349.]

Before going further, dear friend, I believe I ought to insert here a remark of St. Chrysostom, which may be applied to the healing of diseases, or the prevention of accidents and scourges by the Sign of the Cross. If, notwithstanding its power, the Sign of the Cross, even when made with good dispositions, does not always cure the one, and ward off the other, it is not because its virtue is wanting, but because it is useful for us to be tried. [Ad Coloss. ii. Homil. ix.]

There is a disease no less painful than leprosy, and much more common; it is the cancer. It cannot resist the power of the Sign of the Cross any more than other infirmities. Hear the following fact, related by St. Augustine, an eye-witness.

"At Carthage," says he, "lived a pious lady named Innocentia, who belonged to the most illustrious family in the city. She had on her breast a cancer, a horrible malady, which the physicians regarded as incurable. It was to be extracted to the very roots, or, in order to procure some slight relief for the patient, liniments must be continually employed. Then, according to Hippocrates, when the malady is evidently mortal, it is useless to make the patient suffer more.

"Her physician, who was an intimate friend of the family,

had concealed nothing from her. Innocentia turned to God by prayer, confiding in Him alone to work her cure. One night near Easter, she was warned in a dream to go to the baptismal font, on the women's side, where the catechumens were waiting, and to cause the Sign of the Cross to be made on the diseased part by the first catechumen that should present herself before her. She obeyed, and was instantly healed.

"The physician who had announced to her that the disease was incurable, finding her perfectly restored, hastened to inquire what remedy she had employed. She related what had taken place. Then with an air of indifference, which made the pious lady fear that the words were not very respectful to Our Lord, the physician replied: 'I expected to hear something extraordinary from you!' But seeing her become very uneasy, he hastened to add: 'Is it extraordinary that the cancer has been cured by Jesus Christ, by Him who raised to life a man who was four days dead?' " [De Civ. Dei, lib. xxii. c. 8.]

Never was a miracle better attested; the whole city was witness to it.

To natural maladies are often added, to the injury of man's health, the attacks of ferocious or venomous beasts. The remedy to those wounds is again the Sign of the Cross.

"The holy anchoret Thalassius," writes Theodoret, "traveling by night, trod accidentally upon a sleeping viper. The reptile awoke, and in its fury plunged its fangs into the sole of his foot. The saint stooped and placed his right hand on the wound. The viper bit it also, and did not spare the left, which hastened to the assistance of the right. Having satiated its rage, and given more than ten bites, the reptile glided into its hole, and left its victim a prey to the intolerable pain. In this circumstance, no more than in any other, the servant of God had not recourse to human remedies. To cure his wounds he employed the remedies of faith, the Sign of the Cross, prayer, and the invocation of the name of the Lord. [In Thalass.]

Master of life, Our Lord is also Master of death. This sovereign empire is found in the Sign of the Cross. See what we read in the life of St. Dominic. Being in Rome, he preached one day in the ancient church of St. Mark. Among his auditors was a Roman lady called Guttadona, who was much devoted to the servant of God. In order to hear the sermon, she had left one of her children, who was sick; at her return she found it dead. Without making any useless show of grief, she took her servants with her, and carried the child to St. Dominic. She met him at the gate of St. Sixtus' convent, placed the child before him, fell at his feet, and with many tears begged him to give her back her son. The saint, moved with compassion, cast himself on his knees, and after a short prayer made the Sign of the Cross on the child, took him by the hand, raised him full of life, and gave him to his mother, recommending her to preserve absolute silence. But in the excess of her joy, the lady published the miracle, and the whole city of Rome was soon informed of it.

Two centuries earlier we find St. John Gualbert. This noble and saintly warrior had pardoned the murderer of his brother. God rewarded him by giving him a religious vocation, and the power of working miracles. The Sign of the Cross became his sword against the demon. Furious at his numerous defeats, the great homicide armed his agents who, during the night attacked the monastery, burned the church, demolished the buildings, and mortally wounded all the religious. The saint hastened to the rescue, and with the Sign of the Cross restored them to life and health. [See his Life.]

You understand, my dear Frederic, that I have given only one or two cases of each malady. Immense volumes would not suffice to contain them all. St. Augustine, St. Chrysostom, St. Cyril, St. Ephrem, St. Gregory of Nyssa, St. Paulinus, and a hundred other witnesses from the East and the West, in every age, prove by thousands of facts that the adorable Sign of Him who came to cure all our maladies, has not ceased to restore sight to the blind, hearing to the deaf, speech to the dumb, health to the sick, and life to the dead.

Look at history. We must either accept it, such as it is, or tear out all its pages and fall into skepticism, or write another more learned and more worthy of credit. Ask your comrades if they feel competent to undertake it; then when it is finished we shall see.

Adieu until to-morrow.

Mgr. J.J. Gaume

Fourteenth Letter

The Sign of the Cross a preservative against all that could injure life or health—It appeases tempests—Extinguishes fire—Protects us against accidents—Opposes a barrier to floods—Causes the waters to return to their bounds—Keeps ferocious beasts at a distance— Preserves from poison, from thunderbolts—Makes creatures the instruments of prodigies

December 9th

My Dear Frederic,

Powerful as is the Sign of the Cross to give health and life, my dear friend, it is not less so to keep at a distance whatever might be injurious to them. Here again we find abundant facts, but the limits of a letter will allow me to cite only a few. Since the original revolt, all the elements, submitted to the influence of the demons, are conjured up against man. Air, fire, water, and what not, wage against him a war, continual and often deadly. A universal weapon has been given us to defend ourselves; it is the Sign of the Cross.

The God, whose voice commanded the winds and the tempests, commands them again by the sign of our redemption. We read in the life of St. Nicetus, bishop of Treves, that when going to his diocese, he fell asleep on board the vessel in which he had taken passage. In the midst of the voyage, a violent wind agitated the waves, the sails were torn, the masts broken, and the vessel seemed ready to sink. The terrified passengers aroused the saint, who tranquilly made the Sign of the Cross over the angry waves, and a calm immediately succeeded the storm. [S. Greg. Puron, *De gloria confess.*, c. xvii.]

According to the belief of the Church, so clearly expressed in the Roman Pontifical, the demon is a great gatherer of clouds.

~ 118 ~

Over the air, his region and that of his innumerable legions, he exercises a particular influence. How many times does he use it to desolate the country, and above all, to throw obstacles in the way of those who work for the destruction of his empire!

Because of the immense crowds that hastened to hear the sermons of St. Vincent Ferrer, one of his most powerful opponents, he was almost always obliged to preach in the open air. In order to hinder the preaching, the demon rarely failed to raise storms, which the saint was obliged to dissipate. One of the most fearful was that which he dissipated by the Sign of the Cross and holy water. It happened in a town of Catalonia, on the feast of the holy apostles, Peter and Paul, after he had celebrated Mass, and before he had taken off the sacerdotal vestments. [Vit. lib. iii.]

Like air, fire obeys the Sign of the Cross. St. Tiburtius, son of the prefect of Rome, was sentenced either to offer incense to idols, or to walk on a bed of fire. The young martyr made the Sign of the Cross, and without the least hesitation advanced into the middle of the burning coals. Standing barefoot on them, he said to the judge: "Now renounce your errors, and acknowledge that there is no other God than ours. Place, if you dare, your hand in boiling water in the name of Jupiter. Let that Jupiter, whom you call your God, prevent you from feeling the burning heat. As for me, I feel as if I were on a bed of roses. [Act. S. Sebast.]

Sulpicius Severus relates as having heard it from St. Martin himself, that one night the chamber in which the Thaumaturgus of the Gauls was reposing, caught fire. Awakening in a fright, the Saint tried to extinguish the flames, which were already consuming his clothing. His efforts were useless. All at once he returned to himself, and no longer thought of extinguishing the fire, or saving himself, but, full of confidence, he made the Sign of the Cross. The flames immediately separated, and forming an arch over his head, permitted him to continue tranquilly his prayer. [Epist. I. ad Euseb. presbyt., et vit. S. Martini, lib. x.]

Let me relate another fact concerning this great bishop.

Martin, the indefatigable enemy of idolatry, had demolished a very famous and ancient pagan temple. He wished also to cut down a pine tree that stood near it, because it was an object of superstition. The chief priest and other pagans opposed him. At length they said to the courageous bishop: "Since you have so much confidence in your God, we will cut down the tree ourselves, on condition that you stand under it when it falls." The condition was accepted.

In the presence of an innumerable crowd, the saint allowed himself to be tied to that side of the tree on which it leaned. His companions were in mortal terror. Meanwhile the tree, half-cut, seemed ready to fall; in another moment, the venerable bishop would have been crushed. What did the man of God do? He calmly raised his hand and made the Sign of the Cross. At the same instant the tree became straight, and as if blown by a violent wind, fell on the contrary side.

A cry of admiration arose from the assembled multitude, nearly all of whom demanded baptism. [Id ubi supra.]

What took place among the Gauls was renewed also in Italy. The venerable abbot, Honoratus, founder of the monastery of Fundi, one day saw that holy asylum, in which dwelt two hundred religious, threatened with total ruin. From the summit of the mountain, at the foot of which the monastery was built, a large rock had been detached, and threatened to crush everything with its weight. The saint hastened to invoke the name of the Lord, and extending his right hand, opposed to the rock the sign of salvation. The enormous mass suddenly stopped in its course, and remained immovable on the side of the mountain; a position which it retains even to this day. [S. Greg. Dial., lib. i. c. 1.]

From the West let us pass to the East. We shall see that the sovereign power of the Sign of the Cross is not limited by difference of climate, nor degrees of latitude or longitude. Let us listen to St. Jerome. "The universal earthquake, which followed the death of Julian the Apostate, caused the seas to overflow their bounds. As if God threatened the world with a second deluge, in which all things should return to their ancient chaos, vessels were left on the tops of mountains, whither the furious billows had carried them. The inhabitants of Epidaurus, seeing the frightful pools of water on the hills, and dreading lest their town should be submerged, as had happened before, went to find the holy old man, St. Hilarion. They placed him at their head, as if they had been going out to combat. Being arrived at the shore, the saint made the Sign of the Cross three times on the sand, and extended his hand towards the raging waters, which were advancing. It is incredible to what a height the sea rose at that sign, and remained so before him. But after having raged for a long time, as if angry at the obstacle opposed to it by Hilarion, its waves subsided and retired, not daring to cross the sacred limits. Epidaurus and the whole country still relate the miracle; mothers tell it to their children, that the memory of it may descend to posterity." [Vit. S. Hilarion, vers. fin.]

The following is a similar, but more recent fact.

The French historian, Mézeray, relates that in 1196, heavy rains caused the rivers and ponds to overflow, and produced an inundation like a veritable deluge. They knew no other means to stay the flood than prayer, public processions, and supplications. They were employed. No sooner was the Sign of the Cross made upon the waters, than they retired within their limits. [Hist. of France, t. ii. p. 135.]

If Moses' rod, which was only the figure of the Sign of the Cross, could divide the waters of the Red Sea and hold them suspended like mountains, why should not that sign itself cause floods to return to their bounds?

Let us return to the immortal Thebaide, and allow me to relate a few other marvels of which its angelic inhabitants were the actors, and the Sign of the Cross the instrument. One of them, Julian, surnamed Sabas, or the white-haired old man, is traversing the barren solitude. On his way he meets an enormous dragon, which casts on him a ravenous look, and opens its horrid jaws to devour him. Without the least emotion, the venerable anchoret slackens his pace, invokes the name of the Lord, makes the Sign of the Cross, and the dragon dies. [Theodoret, Relig. Hist. c. 2.]

A little later, behold Marcian, a solitary of Syria, who renews the same miracle. While he is praying at the door of the cell, Eusebius, his disciple, who is at a little distance from him, sees a monstrous reptile on the wall at the east side, ready to spring on the saint to devour him. Eusebius, horrified, cries out with all his strength, conjuring his master to fly. Marcian reproves him for his fear, makes the Sign of the Cross, blowing it towards the fearful monster. Behold the effects of the primitive words: "I will put enmity between her seed and thine." The breath which comes from the mouth of the saint is like a flame, which burns the dragon so much, that it falls in pieces like a reed burned by fire. [Ibid. 3.]

It would be easy to multiply instances of facts accomplished in those ever-celebrated places. But that we may group together wonders of the same nature, let us come to Italy, even if we be compelled to return to the East. St. Gregory the Great, relates that St. Amantius, a priest of Citta di Castello, in Umbria, had such power over the most venomous and terrible serpents that they could not live before him. With one Sign of the Cross he caused all those around him to perish. When they went into their holes, he sealed them in with the Sign of the Cross, and afterwards they were taken out dead, killed by an invisible power. Thus has been accomplished the words of the Master, "*serpentes tollent*: (they shall kill serpents)." [Dialog., lib. iii. c. 35.]

You know that Our Lord immediately adds: "*et si mortiferum quid biberint non eis nocebit*: (and if they shall drink any deadly thing, it shall not hurt them)." [St. Mark XVI, 18] I will give a few proofs from among thousands. St. Julian was bishop of the city of Bosra in Idumea. Out of hatred of his religion, some of the principal inhabitants formed a plot to poison him. They bribed the bishop's servant, procured poison and charged him to put it in his master's cup. The unhappy man obeyed.

Being divinely instructed to all that had passed, the saint took the cup, placed it before him, and without touching its contents said to his servant: "Go, in my name, and invite the principal inhabitants of the city to dine with me." He knew that among them should be found the guilty ones. All accepted the invitation. Then the holy man, being unwilling to expose any one, said with angelic sweetness: "As it is your wish to poison the humble Julian, here is the poison, I am going to drink it." He made the Sign of the Cross three times over the cup, saying, "In the name of the Father, and of the Son, and of the Holy Ghost, I drink this cup." He drained it to the last drop and received no injury. At this sight, his enemies fell at his feet and begged his pardon. [Sophron., in Prat. spir.]

One must be a Bachelor of the nineteenth century to be ignorant of the following fact.

If there is a man whose life should be known in its minutest details, it is St. Benedict, the patriarch of the Western monks. Like another Moses, is it not by him and his children that Europe has been drawn from barbarism? Show us a piece of waste land, either moral or material, that the Benedictine has not cultivated; a civilizing principle that he has not matured, taught, practiced, at the price of efforts which God alone knows.

What we do know is that satan, the old Pharaoh, left no means untried to hinder the benevolent work. No sooner had Benedict retired into his solitude than he beheld coming to him a few monks unworthy of the name; they asked to be taken under his care. The saint gave them a rule, and by word as well as example, endeavored to bring them under the yoke of regular discipline.

Vain effort! Example wounded their pride, words provoked their anger, and aroused their hatred. They took a resolution to poison their venerable superior. They mixed poison in the wine, and filled a glass with it, which they presented to him, that he might bless it, according to the custom of the monastery. Benedict stretched forth his hand, made the Sign of the Cross, and by this sacred sign, as by the blow of a stone, the poisoned glass was shivered into fragments. The saint understood that they had presented him with the cup of death, from which he had been preserved by the Sign of the Cross. [S. Greg. lib. ii, c. 3.]

From these examples, and a thousand others, you may see, dear friend, what a powerful prayer is the Sign of the Cross, with how many graces it enriches us, and from how many dangers it preserves our frail existence.

Let us come now to another application of the protecting sign.

In France, Spain, Italy and, I believe in your own country, Catholics are accustomed to make the Sign of the Cross when it thunders and lightens. Those who doubt nothing, take this for weakness, as if the true Catholics of the eighteen centuries which have preceded us, were all weak-minded persons and superstitious women.

Now, in the circumstances indicated above, and in all unforeseen dangers, we find the Sign of the Cross in use among the Christians of the East and the West, from the first ages of the Church. St. Ephrem, St. Augustine, St. Gregory of Tours, and a thousand other witnesses, have seen it in our stead, and affirm it.

"If, on a sudden," says the deacon of Edessa, "the lightning flashes from the clouds, and the thunder bursts with a crash, man is terror-stricken and all in fear, we bow ourselves to the earth."*

Speaking of those who frequent worldly assemblies, St. Augustine adds: "If, by chance, anything affright them, they immediately make the Sign of the Cross." [Lib 50. Homil., homil. 21.]

St. Gregory relates as a thing of public notoriety, that under the impression of fear, or at the approach of any danger

---

* Ser. de cruce. The saint speaks of the Sign of the Cross, and though he does not name it, it is clear that it was made in this circumstance, since they never failed to make it in even the most ordinary actions.

whatsoever, the Christians had recourse to this sign, their protector. And not in vain; among thousands we choose the following proof.

Two men were journeying from Geneva to Lausanne. They were soon overtaken by a violent storm, accompanied with vivid lightning and repeated claps of thunder. According to the traditional custom of Christians, one of the travelers made the Sign of the Cross on himself. The other scoffed at him, and said: "Are you chasing the flies? Leave those superstitions to old women. Such mummeries are a disgrace to religion, and unworthy of an intelligent man." [Lib. ii. Miracul. S. Martin, c. 45]

He had scarcely finished speaking, when a thunderbolt stretched him dead at the feet of his companion.

Then the first, more than ever, continued to protect himself by the Sign of the Cross. His journey was happily terminated, and he related everywhere what had happened to him. [Tilman, Collect. of the Holy Fathers, Book vii. c. 58.]

A warning to the strong-minded, who are secured against thunderbolts.

The Sign of the Cross protects not only the life of man, but is also a pledge of security for all that belongs to him. Thence comes the universal use of this liberating sign over houses, fields, fruits and animals.

"Catholics" says the grave Stuckius, "have prayers, accompanied by the Sign of the Cross, for every creature in particular; water, leaves, flowers, the Paschal lamb, milk, honey, cheese, bread, vegetables, eggs, wine, oil, and the vessels that contain them. In each formula they ask expressly for the removal of the malicious power of the demon, and health for body and soul.

"On the day of the Resurrection, they bless milk, honey,

meat, eggs, loaves of bread, everything that they keep or give, as being salutary for the soul. On the day of the Assumption, herbs, plants, roots and the fruit of trees, to communicate to them a divine virtue.

"On St. John's day, wine without which this blessing they regard as impure and the principle of evil. On St. Stephen's, the pastures, on St. Mark's, the grain. In this they follow the precept of St. Paul, who bids the faithful bless all that is used for the support of life, and return thanks for them:—mysterious usages for which theologians give excellent reasons." [Antiq. convivial., lib. ii. c. 36. p. 430.]

In their turn, those creatures, delivered from the influence of the demon, become, thanks to the Sign of the Cross, instruments of the powerful goodness of the Creator.

We read in St. Gregory of Tours, that a pestilential malady made such ravages among cattle, that people began to ask themselves if the species would not become wholly extinct. In their desolation, some country people came to the basilica of St. Martin, and took thence holy water and the oil from the lamps. Having carried it to their homes they made the Sign of the Cross with it on the heads of the cattle who had not as yet been attacked, and gave it as a drink to those who were at the point of expiring; all were instantly cured. [Lib. iii., Mirac. S. Mart. c. xviii.]

Let us cite a last example of the protecting power of the Sign of the Cross. St. Germanus, bishop of Paris, was on his way to meet the relics of St. Symphorian, Martyr. As he was passing by a village, the inhabitants came and begged him to take pity on a poor woman named Panitia, whose little field of wheat was ravaged by bears. "Come," said they to him, "come, and look at that poor field, so that the malicious beasts may fly from your presence."

Notwithstanding the opposition of those that accompanied him, the saint went to the place, and made the Sign of the Cross over the little hermitage. Very soon two bears came to the spot; transported with fury, they fell upon each other; one was left dead upon the field, the other being mortally wounded, was dispatched with a spear, and the poor widow had never again occasion to deplore the loss of her harvest. [Fortunat. In Vit. S. Germ.]

History abounds in similar facts, but let this suffice for to-day.

Mgr. J. J. Gaume

Fifteenth Letter

Answer to a question—The Sign of the Cross is a weapon which repulses the enemy—Life is a warfare—Against whom?—Necessity of a weapon within the reach of every one—What is that weapon?—Proofs that the Sign of the Cross is the special weapon, the most forcible weapon against the evil spirits

December 10th

My Dear Frederic,

If you communicate my last letter to your companions, it is probable, my dear friend, that they will say to you: "If the Sign of the Cross is as powerful as he writes to you, why does it no longer do what it has done?"

To this question there are many answers.

The first is given by St. Augustine. In speaking of miracles, the great doctor makes a very just observation. "The miracles," says he, "recorded in the holy books, have a great publicity. As everybody reads or hears them read, no one is ignorant of them. This is as it should be, because they are the proofs of faith.

"To-day, also, miracles are operated in the name of the Lord, by the sacraments, by prayers, and at the tombs of the saints, but they are far from having the same notoriety as the first. They are known in the places where they are wrought, but if it be in a considerable city, they will scarcely be known to all; nay, it often happens that but very few are informed of them. When they relate them to others or in other places, the authority of their testimony is not such as to be admitted without difficulty or hesitation; although they be related by Christians to other Christians." [De civ. Dei, lib. xvii.]

In proof what he advances, the saint relates many miracles operated under his eyes, some of them by the Sign of the Cross.

Therefore, because your companions or other persons know not the miracles accomplished in our day by the Sign of the Cross, there is no reason to conclude that it operates them no longer.

To this first answer, a second naturally links itself. It is from another great doctor, Pope St. Gregory. Distinguishing former times from the present, he says: "At the beginning of the Church, miracles were necessary. It was by them that the faith of the people was confirmed. When we plant a tree, we water it until it takes root. As soon as we are assured that it will grow, the watering is stopped. This is what the apostle says: 'The gift of tongues is a sign, not for the faithful, but for infidels.' " [Homil. xxix. in Evang.]

It is the same with moral improvement as with material. Now that Christianity has taken root even in the bowels of the earth, miracles are not as necessary as at the time of the divine planting. Already fifteen hundred years have rolled away since St. Augustine said: "He who in our days asks prodigies in order to believe, is himself the greatest of prodigies." [Ubi supra.]

For a moment replace the world in the same circumstances as it was at the birth of the Church, and you shall see the Sign of the Cross renewing all its primitive miracles. Listen to contemporary history.

"Would you believe it?" writes one of our missionary bishops, "ten villages are converted! The demon is furious, and strikes a hundred blows. During the fifteen days that I have been preaching, there have been five or six possessions. With holy water and the Sign of the Cross, our catechumens expel the devils, and cure the sick. I have seen some marvelous things. The devil helps me very much to convert the pagans. As in the time of Our Lord, although the father of lies, he cannot prevent himself from telling the truth.

"Behold this poor man, possessed with an evil spirit, making a thousand contortions, and crying out: 'Why do you preach the true religion? I cannot endure that you should take away all my disciples.' 'What is your name?' asks the catechist. After some refusals, he answers: 'I am the envoy of Lucifer.' 'How many are you?' 'Twenty-two.' Holy water and the Sign of the Cross delivered the possessed." [Letter of Mgr. Anouilh, Bishop of Abydos, missionary in China. Tching-Ting-Fou, province of Peking, March 12th, 1862.]

But even admitting, which I do not, that the Sign of the Cross no longer works miracles among Christian people, by how many superhuman effects does it not reveal its power at each hour of the day and night, throughout Christendom? If we suppose one hundred million temptations in the day, we may hold it for a certainty that more than three-fourths of them are dissipated by the Sign of the Cross. Who has not had experience of this in himself? Judge from this; and remember that what you do, others do also; you may by this estimate the universal and permanent power of the Sign of the Cross, the liberator.

I will go further, and admit that the Sign of the Cross does not always succeed in chasing away importunate thoughts, in dispelling seductive charms, or in withdrawing the soul from the verge of the abyss; but with whom lies the fault? Is it not on account of the little faith of the Christians of our day? Must we not say, with regard to the inefficacy of the Sign of the Cross, what we, with good reason, say of the fruitlessness of Holy Communion in a great number—that the fault is not in the food, but in the disposition of him that eats: *Defectus non in cibo est, sed in edentis dispositione* (the fault is not in the food, but in the disposition of those eating)?

It is with a view to cure this want of faith, which impoverishes and ruins Christians, that I have undertaken this correspondence. I shall continue it by developing another title which the Sign of the Cross possesses, to the confidence of the Catholics of the nineteenth century.

THEY ARE SOLDIERS, THE SIGN OF THE CROSS IS A WEAPON WHICH REPULSES THE ENEMY.

More than three thousand years have elapsed since Job defined the life of man to be a continual warfare: *militia est vita hominis super terram* (The life of man upon earth is a warfare). [Job VII, 1] Ages have rolled away, generations have succeeded generations, empires have given place to other empires; twenty times has the face of the world been renewed, yet Job's definition has always remained true.

Life is a warfare; a warfare for you as well as for me, as for your companions, for the rich as well as the poor. It is a warfare begun at the cradle, to end only at the tomb; a warfare for every moment of the night and day, in sickness and in health. It is a decisive warfare; on the victory depends not fortune, health, nor the temporal advantages we esteem so highly, but infinitely more than all those—an eternity of happiness, or an eternity of woe.

Such, my dear friend, is man's condition here below; we can change nothing of it. Who are his enemies, yours, mine? Ah! who is there that does not know them, not only by name, but by their attacks? The devil, the world, and the flesh; three formidable enemies, bent on our ruin. As I have not the slightest idea of giving you a complete course of asceticism, I shall occupy myself only with the first.

As sure as there is a God, so sure also there are demons.

"No satan, no God," said Voltaire, and he was right. If there is no satan, there was no fall, no redemption, no Christianity; no Christianity, all is false; the human race is foolish, and there is no God.

Now, the demons are fallen angels. By their intelligence, strength and agility, they are far superior to man. Their number is incalculable. Until the day of the last judgment, they have for their abode the atmosphere which surrounds us. Jealous of the sons of Adam for being called to enjoy the happiness they have lost, their occupation both day and night is to lay snares for us; to excite our passions, to cause us to be placed in dangerous positions, to obscure in us our esteem for the faith, to stifle remorse, and to blunt our moral sense, in order to make us the accomplices of their revolt, the companions of their torments. All these truths are, I repeat, as certain as the existence of God.

Tyrants over man by sin, the demons are also such over creatures subject to man; the king being vanquished, all his subjects belong to the victor.

Distributed throughout all parts of the creation, and in each creature in particular, they penetrate them with their malignant influence. Within the limits of the power that has been given them, they make it the instrument of their hatred against man, against his soul and body. This is also a dogma of universal belief.

What does he know, who is ignorant of this? Nothing. And he who doubts it? Less than nothing. He who denies it, deserves no longer to be numbered among intelligent beings.

Now the struggle and man being given such as they are, can you conceive it possible that Divine Wisdom would have left mankind without defense? Must you not, on the contrary, understand as clearly as that two and two make four, that in order to equalize the struggle, God has given to man a powerful, a universal weapon, always at hand and within the reach of every one. What is this weapon?

Let us ask all ages, particularly Christian ages. With unanimous voice they answer, that it is the Sign of the Cross. The constant use which they have made of it gives the answer. This point of view illuminates all the history of the Sign of the Cross. It highly justifies the conduct of the primitive Christians, and no less highly condemns our own. There is nothing more certain than that this sign is the especial weapon, the powerful weapon against satan and his angels. Tell me— when we want to know the value of a cannon, a carbine, or any other arm of new invention, in what way do we proceed?

We do not blindly trust to the inventor. The authorities name a committee; the weapon is tried in presence of competent judges. The judgment which they form decides the value of the engine of war submitted to their examination.

Let it be the same with the Sign of the Cross; only remember that the divine sign is not a weapon of new invention. It is old, very old, but it is neither rusty, nor weak, nor worn out.

As to the committee of examination, it has been long formed, and leaves nothing to be desired. It is composed of the ablest men of the East and the West; chosen men, who, from ancient times have known the weapon in question, and the details of the warfare, not only in theory but in practice. Behold the tribunal; let us hear its judgment.

Does that judge believe in the power of the Sign of the Cross, and the fitness of that divine weapon to combat with the demons, who expresses his decision in the following terms: "Never leave your house without making the Sign of the Cross.

It will be to you a staff, a weapon, an impregnable fortress. Neither man nor demon will dare to attack you, seeing you covered with such powerful armor. Let this sign teach you yourself that you are a soldier, ready to combat against the demons, and ready to fight for the crown of justice. Are you ignorant of what the Cross has done? It has vanquished death, destroyed sin, emptied hell, dethroned satan, and resuscitated the universe; would you then doubt its power?" [S. Chrys. Homil. xxii. ad popul. Antioch.]

Does that second judge believe in it, who says: "The Sign of the Cross is the invincible armor of the Christian. Soldier of Christ, let this armor never leave you, either day or night, at any moment, or in any place. Without it, undertake nothing. Whether you be asleep or awake, watching or working, eating or drinking, sailing on sea or crossing rivers, have this breast-plate ever on you. Adorn and protect each of your members with this victorious sign, and nothing can injure you. There is no buckler so powerful against the darts of the enemy. At the sight of this sign, the infernal powers, affrighted and trembling, take to flight." [S. Eph., De Panoplia et de Pœnitent. apud Gretzer. pp. 580, 581, 642.]

Does that third judge believe in it, who addresses to himself and to all Christians the following recommendation: "Let us make the Sign of the Cross boldly and courageously. When the demons see it, they are reminded of the Crucified; they take to flight; they hide themselves and leave us." [S. Cyril. Catech. xiii.]

And the fourth, who says: "Let us bear on our foreheads the immortal standard. The sight of it makes the demons tremble. They who fear not the gilded capitols, tremble at the sight of the Cross." [Orig. Homil. vii. in divers Evang. locis.]

Thus has the East decided by the voice of her greatest men,

St. Chrysostom, St. Ephrem, St. Cyril of Jerusalem, and Origen, to which it would be easy to add other names equally respectable.

Let us hearken to the West.

St. Augustine says to the catechumens: "It is with the symbol and the Sign of the Cross that we must march to meet the enemy. Clothed with this armor, the Christian shall easily triumph over his proud and ancient tyrant. The Cross is sufficient to cause all the machinations of the spirits of darkness to vanish." [Lib. de Symb. c. i.]

His illustrious contemporary, St. Jerome, says: "The Sign of the Cross is a buckler which shields us from the burning arrows of the demon."

And elsewhere: "Frequently make the Sign of the Cross on your forehead, that you may not yield to the destroyer of Egypt." [Ep. xviii, ad Eustoch and Epist. 97 ad Demetriad]

And Lactantius says: "Whoever wishes to know the power of the Sign of the Cross, has only to consider how formidable it is to the demons. When adjured in the name of Jesus Christ, it forces them to leave the bodies of the possessed. What is there in this to wonder at? When the Son of God was on earth, with one word He put the demons to flight, and restored peace and health to their unfortunate victims. To-day His disciples expel those same unclean spirits in the name of their Master, and by the sign of His passion." [Lib. iv. c. 27.]

The East and the West have spoken. The most able judges proclaim the Sign of the Cross to be an excellent weapon, a special weapon against the demons. An incalculable number of facts form the basis of their judgment. In the first ages of the Church they were repeated every day in the presence of Christians and pagans, in all places of the universe.

They were so conclusive that St. Athanasius, an eye-witness, said without fear of any contradiction: "By the Sign of the Cross all the arts of magic are rendered powerless, all enchantments inefficacious; and all idols deserted. By it the passions of the sensual voluptuaries are moderated, checked and appeased; and the soul groveling on the earth, is raised towards heaven.

"Formerly the demons deceived men by assuming divers forms, and standing near a fountain or a river; in the woods or upon rocks, and by their enchantments and by delusions surprised unwary mortals. But since the advent of the Divine Word, their artifices are powerless; the Sign of the Cross is able to unmask all their impostures.

"Does any one wish to prove it? He needs only to come into the midst of the enchantments of the demons, the impostures of the oracles, and the miracles of magic; then let him make the Sign of the Cross and invoke the name of the Lord, and he shall see how, through fear of the sacred sign, the demons will fly, the oracles become dumb, the charms and incantations be struck powerless." [Lib. de Incarnat. Verb.]

I will relate a few of those experiences. Lactantius, the preceptor of Constantine's son, who knew better than any one the secrets of the imperial court, relates the following.

"While in the East, the Emperor Maximian, a very curious searcher into the future, one day immolated some victims, and sought to read in their entrails the secrets of the future. Some of his guards who were Christians, made on their foreheads the *immortale signum*: (immortal sign). At the same moment the demons fled away, and the sacrifice became dumb." [Lactant. De mortib perse., c. x.]

If, at the sight of the Sign of the Cross, the demon was

obliged to fly away from his temples, how could he remain in other places? Let us hear one of the most grave doctors of the East, St. Gregory of Nyssa.

In the life of St. Gregory Thaumaturgus, the Moses of Armenia, the illustrious historian relates what follows.

"Troades, his deacon, arrived one evening at Neocæsarea. Being fatigued with his journey, he wished to take a bath, in order to refresh himself, and for this purpose went to the public baths. That place was haunted by a murderous demon, who killed all those who dared to enter there after nightfall, therefore the doors were closed at sunset. The deacon presented himself and requested to have them opened. The keeper of the bath told him all that had happened. 'You may believe me,' said he, 'whoever dares to enter here at this hour, never comes forth alive. At night the demon is master of the place, and many unfortunate persons have paid for their temerity by cries of agony and by death.' Troades was not moved by what he heard, but insisted on the doors being opened. Overcome by his solicitations, the keeper of the bath bethought himself of an expedient by which he might save his own life and at the same time satisfy the desire of the petitioner. He gave him the keys, not daring to open the door himself, and ran away. The deacon entered alone. Arrived in the first room, he began to remove his clothes. All at once, and on every side, objects of horror and dread, spectres of various forms, half flame, half smoke, figures of men and beasts, presented themselves to his sight, howled in his ears, infected him with their loathsome breath, and surrounded him as with a circle that could not be broken. Without the least emotion, the deacon made the Sign of the Cross, invoked the name of the Lord, and left the first room in safety. Having entered the bath-room, he found himself in the midst of a more horrible spectacle. The demon appeared to him under a form calculated to cause the death of any one by terror. The earth shook, the walls were rent asunder, the floor opened and the deacon saw beneath him a furnace, from which the sparks flew into his face. He had recourse to his former weapon, the Sign of the Cross, and the invocation of the name of the Lord, and all disappeared. After having taken his bath he hastened to depart, but the demon barred his passage and kept the doors closed. But by the Sign of the Cross, satan's opposition was again overcome, and the door flew open of itself. As the courageous deacon went forth, the demon said to him in a *humana vox*, (human voice): 'Do not imagine it owing to your virtue that you have escaped death. You owe it to Him whose name you invoked.' Having thus been saved, Troades became a subject of admiration to the keeper of the bath, and to all those who knew of the occurrence." [Vit. B. Greg. Inter oper, Nyssa.]

The fact that you have just read, dear friend, is not an isolated one. It is but a part of a vast whole of similar facts, attested by thousands of witnesses in past ages, which are reproduced in our days amongst idolaters. Rome often witnessed them. Allow Lactantius to speak.

"When the pagans," says he, "sacrifice to their gods, if any of the assistants marks his forehead with the Sign of the Cross, the sacrifice cannot take place, and the oracle consulted gives no answer. Such has often been the cause why wicked emperors have persecuted the Christians. Some of us accompanying them to the sacrifices, have made the Sign of the Cross; then the demons, being put to flight, could not mark in the entrails of the victims the signs indicative of the future. When the pagan priests perceived this, they failed not, being incited thereto by the demons to whom they sacrificed, to complain of the presence of the profane. The princes became furious, and persecuted Christianity to the extreme, that it might defile itself with sacrileges of which they so cruelly bore the pain." [Lact. lib. iv. c. 27.]

My next shall contain some other facts.

Mgr. J. J. Gaume

Sixteenth Letter

The Sign of the Cross breaks idols and expels the demons from them: examples—It expels them from the possessed: examples—Recent anecdote—Other proofs: exorcisms—It renders vain the direct attacks of the demons: examples—Their indirect attacks: proofs—All creatures subject to the demons serve as their instruments to harm us—The Sign of the Cross delivers them, and prevents their being injurious to our body or soul—Profound Philosophy of the early Christians—The use they made of the Sign of the Cross—Tableau by St. Chrysostom

December 11th

My Dear Frederic,

The power of the Sign of the Cross, my dear Frederic, must be as extended as that of satan. The infernal usurper has seized upon all parts of creation; the legitimate proprietor has, then, to eject him, and to give to those who have the use of them the means by which to eject him themselves. Therefore not only does the Sign of the Cross prevent the demons from speaking, and oblige them to leave the places they inhabit, but it also expels them from the bodies of the possessed. I shall give a few facts from among thousands in support of these self-evident truths.

The following happened under the Emperor Antoninus. That Cæsar, the philosopher, cruelly persecuted the faithful. Rome was filled with idols. To their feet they dragged our ancestors, to compel them to offer incense. Glyceria, one of our heroic sisters, was brought before the governor of the imperial city. "Take this torch," said he, "and sacrifice to Jupiter." "I will never do so," answered Glyceria. "I sacrifice to the eternal God; for that I need no torch, which produces smoke. Cause it to be extinguished, that my sacrifice may be the more agreeable to Him." The governor spoke, and the torches were extinguished. Then the chaste and noble virgin raised her eyes towards heaven, and stretching forth her hands towards the people, said: "Do you see the brilliant torch engraven on my forehead?" At these words she made the Sign of the Cross and prayed: "O Almighty God, whom Thy servants glorify by the Cross of Jesus Christ, break this demon formed by the hand of man." At the same moment a clap of thunder resounded in their ears, and the marble Jupiter was shattered into fragments." [Baron. t. ii.]

We read the same of St. Procopius, a martyr under Diocletian. Being brought before the idols, the glorious champion stood facing the East, and made the Sign of the Cross over his body. Then, raising his eyes and hands to heaven, he said, "O Lord Jesus Christ!" making at the same time the Sign of the Cross against the statues, and accompanying it with the words: "Impure images, I say to you, fear the name of my God: melt now into water, and spread over this temple." His words were immediately accomplished. [Sur. 8. Jul.]

Obliged by the Sign of the Cross to quit the places they inhabit, the demons are equally constrained, by virtue of the same sign, to leave the bodies of the unfortunates of whom they have taken possession. Here again we find numerous facts attested by unexceptionable witnesses.

First, there is St. Gregory, one of the greatest popes that have governed the Catholic Church. He speaks of a fact of recent occurrence in his own country. "In the time of the Goths," says he, "King Totila came to Narni. [A small town not far from Rome.] The town had for its bishop the venerable Cassius, who thought he had better go to meet the prince. The habit of weeping had inflamed the face of the holy bishop, but Totila, judging it to be the effect of wine-drinking, showed a profound contempt for the man of God. But the Almighty wished to show how great was he of whom so little account was made. In the plain of Narni, and in sight of the entire army, the demon took possession of Totila's squire, and cruelly tormented him. In presence of the king, they brought him to the venerable Cassius. The saint began to pray, made the Sign of the Cross, and the demon was expelled. From that moment Totila's contempt was changed into respect, he having learned the true character of him whose appearance had excited his contempt. [Dialog., lib. iii., c. 6.]

Listen to another fact which took place in your own country. In Prussia, in a place called Velsenberg, there lived a rich and powerful man called Ethelbert. He was possessed by a demon, and had to be bound with iron chains. As he was a prey to most cruel pains, he received many visits. One day, in presence of the priests of the idols and many pagans, the demon cried out: "If Swibert, the servant of the living God, does not come, I will never depart hence."

You are not ignorant that St. Swibert was one of the apostles of Friesland and part of Germany. As the demon unceasingly repeated the same words, the idolaters went away much puzzled, not knowing what to think of all that they had seen and heard. After much hesitation, his friends decided to seek the saint. Having found him, they earnestly entreated him to visit the demoniac. Swibert consented. Scarcely had he set out, when the possessed man began to foam at the mouth, to gnash his teeth, and to scream more horribly than ever. As the saint drew near his dwelling, he suddenly became calm and tranquil, and lay on his bed as if in a peaceful sleep.

The saint, having looked at him, bade his companions to

pray. He himself conjured the Lord, that for the glory of His name, and the conversion of the unbelievers, He would expel the demon from the body of the unfortunate man. When his prayer was ended, he arose and made the Sign of the Cross over the demoniac, saying: "In the Name of Our Lord Jesus Christ, I command thee, impure spirit, to depart out of this creature of God, that he may know Him who is truly his Creator." At that instant the evil spirit went out, leaving behind him a horrid stench. [Marcellin., in Vit. S. Suibert., c. xx.] The sick man, overwhelmed with joy, fell at the saint's feet, and with tears begged for baptism, which was granted him.

Behold, dear Frederic, what was happening in Prussia when she was drawn out of barbarism. There, as in other places, it was by miracles that the Gospel proved its mission, and the Sign of the Cross was its ordinary instrument. What is now the religion of the Prussians? Is it that of the first apostles? That which teaches to make the Sign of the Cross?

The Protestants unceasingly cry out that an honest man ought not to change his religion. They love, say they, men who hold to the religion of their fathers; as for me, I love those better who hold to that of their grandfathers. You know, no doubt, the anecdote related of the celebrated Count de Stolberg. This amiable and learned man, one of the glories of your Germany, had abjured Protestantism. The king of Prussia was highly displeased, and refused to see him. However, after the lapse of some years, the king being desirous of his advice, sent for the count. As soon as they met, William said to him: "Sir Count, I cannot conceal that I have but little esteem for a man who changes his religion." The Count bowing, replied: "This is the very reason, Sire, why I so profoundly despise Luther."

That the Sign of the Cross is the universal and all-powerful weapon, with which to expel the demons from the bodies of the possessed, is proved by the exorcisms of the Church. If you cast a glance over the Roman Ritual, you will find the proof of what I advance. Now the exorcisms, with the breathings and the Sign of the Cross, date back to the very cradle of Christianity. Mention is made of it by all the Fathers who have spoken of Baptism, and nearly every one both in the East and the West has spoken of it.

In the name of all, let us hear St. Gregory the Great.

"When the catechumens present themselves to be exorcised, the priest must first breathe on the face, in order that the demon, being ejected, entrance may be given to Jesus Christ, our God. Then, he makes the Sign of the Cross on the forehead, saying: 'I place on thy forehead the Sign of the Cross of Our Lord Jesus Christ;' and on the breast, saying: 'I place on thy breast the sign of Our Lord Jesus Christ.' " [S. Greg. Sacrament.]

The exorcisms, as above described, have descended to us through all ages. At this very hour they are still in use in every part of the globe where there is a Catholic priest on mission, and a human being to be withdrawn from the dominion of satan. But the demons are not only in the temples and statues wherein they are worshipped, or in the bodies of the unfortunates whom they torment; they are everywhere. The air is full of them. They are indefatigable enemies, who continually attack us, either by themselves, or through the intermediation of creatures. Their attacks, whether direct or indirect, open or masked, fail before the Sign of the Cross. "The Lord," says Arnobius, "has prepared our fingers for the combat, so that when we shall be attacked by our enemies, visible or invisible, we may use our fingers to form on our foreheads the triumphant Sign of the Cross." [Arnob. in ps. 143.]

Among thousands of other heroines, as young and exposed as she, Justina of Nicomedia knew how to employ this victorious weapon. Born of noble parents, endowed with riches and rare beauty, the young Christian virgin, notwithstanding her modesty and her flight from the world, inspired a young pagan named Agladius with a violent passion. To attain his desires, he employed offers, promises and prayers, but finding all useless, had recourse to Cyprian, a famous magician in the city. He soon experienced the same passion, and employed all the resources of his art to win her for himself. He had no difficulty in obtaining the aid of hell. The most violent demons were sent to tempt the young saint. Finding herself so strongly attacked, Justina redoubled her prayers, watchings and mortifications. In the height of the combat she made the Sign of the Cross, and the demons took to flight. Not only did she preserve her virtue, but she had also the glory of converting Cyprian, who became an illustrious martyr, and one of the most noble conquest of the liberating sign. [Life, Sept. 26th.]

And St. Anthony, the great champion of the desert, whose life was spent in warfare with the demons, in their paroxysms of rage and under the most frightful forms, he also knew how to handle this victorious weapon. Let a historian worthy of such a man speak.

"Sometimes," says St. Athanasius, "a sudden noise was heard. Anthony's dwelling shook violently, and through the half-opened walls poured in a crowd of demons, who assumed the forms of beasts and serpents. The cell was filled with lions, bulls, wolves, asps, dragons, scorpions, bears and leopards, each of which uttered its natural cry. The lion roared, ready to devour him; the bull threatened with his bellowing and his horns; the serpent hissed; the wolf showed his teeth; the leopard, by his variegated colors, represented the cunning of the infernal serpent: all were frightful to behold, horrible to hear.

"Anthony, beaten and wounded, suffered acute pain in his body, but his soul remained imperturbable. Though his wounds drew from him moans of pain, nevertheless he, ever the same, cried out derisively to his enemies: 'If you had any strength, one of you alone could vanquish me, but because the power of my God enfeebles you, you come in crowds to frighten me.' He added: 'If you have any power, if my God has delivered me to you, here I am, devour me. If you can do nothing against me, why do you make so many useless efforts? The Sign of the Cross, and confidence in God, are for us an impregnable fortress.' Then they gnashed their teeth, and uttered a thousand threats against the saint, seeing that their attacks only served to bring derision on themselves." [De vit. S. Anton.]

The same fearless language which faith caused Anthony to use towards the demons, was also addressed by him to the pagan philosophers. "What is the use of disputations?" said the patriarch of the desert to those perpetual seekers after truth. "We pronounce the name of the Crucified, and all the demons that you adore as gods, howl and roar. At the first Sign of the Cross, they fly from the possessed. Behold! where are the lying oracles? Where the enchantments of the Egyptians? Of what use are magic words? All have been destroyed since that day when the name of Jesus Crucified resounded through the world." Then having called to him some who were possessed, he continued to say to his interlocutors: "Come on with your syllogisms, or any other charm that you please. Expel out of these miserable victims those whom you call your gods. If you cannot, then confess yourselves vanquished. Have recourse to the Sign of the Cross, and the humility of your faith shall be followed by a miracle of power." At these words he invoked the name of Jesus, made the Sign of the Cross over the foreheads of the possessed, and the demons fled, in presence of the confounded philosophers. [Ibid.]

Similar facts are almost as numerous as the pages of history. You know them, and I will pass on.

To attacks, direct and palpable, the demons add those that are masked and indirect. Not less dangerous than the first, they are much more frequent. They are of two kinds; one, interior; the other, exterior. The first are what we commonly call temptations. Now I have said that the Sign of the Cross is the victorious arm which disperses them, and in saying it, I am only the echo of universal tradition and daily experience.

"When you make the Sign of the Cross," says St. Chrysostom, "remember what the cross signifies, and you shall appease anger and all the inordinate motions of the soul." [De ador. pret. cruc., n. 3.]

Origen adds: "Such is the power of the Sign of the Cross, that if you place it before your eyes, if you keep it faithfully in your heart, neither concupiscence, nor voluptuousness, nor fury can resist it; at its appearance the whole army of flesh and sin take flight. [Origen, Comm. in epist. ad Rom. lib. vi. n. 6.]

The second attacks are exterior. Not a creature escapes the malignant influence of satan, and he makes them all the instruments of his implacable hatred against man. This is, as I have already demonstrated, an article of belief among mankind.

What weapon has God given (for He has given one) to free them, and by freeing them, to preserve our souls and bodies from the fatal injuries of him who is justly styled the great Homicide, *Homicida ab initio*, (He was a murderer from the beginning)? [St. John VIII, 44] All Catholic generations rise from their tombs to cry out to me: "It is the Sign of the Cross." All those now living in the five divisions of the globe, join their voice to that of their ancestors and repeat: It is the Sign of the Cross."

Impenetrable buckler, impregnable tower, special defense against the demons, universal weapon, equally powerful against the visible and the invisible enemy, weapon easy for the weak, gratuitous for the poor:—such is, as we have seen, the definition which both the living and the dead give us of the adorable sign. Hence two great truths; the subjection of all creatures to the demons, and the power of the Sign of the Cross to free them, and prevent them from injuring us. From these two truths, so deeply felt; these truths, ever ancient, yet ever new, arise two facts incontestably logical. The first, the constant use of exorcisms in the Catholic Church; the second, the incessant use of the Sign of the Cross among the primitive Christians.

What is the meaning of exorcism? The faith of the Church applied to the servitude of creatures to the demon. What does exorcism operate? The deliverance of creatures. Then as there is not a creature that the Catholic Church does not exorcise, the result is, that in her eyes the universe in all its parts is a great captive, possessed by the demon, an immense engine of war directed against us. What, in its turn, was the Sign of the Cross among the early Christians? A continual exorcism. If, with the Church, and mankind, we admit that all creatures are subject to the demon, that they serve as vehicles for his malignant influence; that at every hour, every instant, every action, man comes in contact with them; what more reasonable than the constant use of an arm, ever and always necessary?

Thus, then, the continual use of the Sign of the Cross among our ancestors announces a profound philosophy. They knew dualism, the great law of the moral world, in all its formidable extent. They understood that the attack being universal and incessant, it was necessary, in order to preserve an equilibrium, that the defense also should be universal and incessant. Again, what is more reasonable? They then made the Sign of the Cross on each of their senses. Do you wish to know why? The senses are the doors of the soul; they serve as intermediary between it and creatures. Once that they are marked with the Sign of the Cross, creatures can no longer enter into communication with the soul, unless by passing through a sanctified medium, in which they lose their fatal influences.

But this was not enough for our forefathers. They made the Sign of the Cross on everything that they used, and even, as far as in their power, on every part of creation. Houses, furniture, doors, fountains, boundaries of fields, pillars of edifices, ships, bridges, medals, flags, helmets, shields, rings; all were marked with the adorable sign. Prevented by their occupations, or by distance of place, from repeating it everywhere and always, they rendered it permanent, as it were, by engraving, painting, or sculpturing it on the creatures in the midst of which they passed their existence. A lightning-rod, a trophy of victory; such then was the august sign. A divine lightning-rod, much more powerful to repulse the princes of the air with their incalculable malice, than the metallic rods placed on our houses are to discharge the lightning clouds. A trophy of victory, attesting the triumph of the Incarnate Word over the king of this world, as the columns raised by the vanquisher on the field of battle bear witness to the defeat of the enemy. From the heights of Constantinople let us, with St. Chrysostom, contemplate the world covered with those divine lightning-rods, those trophies of victory.

"More precious than the universe," says the eloquent patriarch, "the Cross glitters on the diadems of emperors. Everywhere it is present to my view. I find it among princes and subjects, men and women, virgins and married people, slaves and freemen. All continually trace it on the noblest part of the body, the forehead, where it shines like a column of glory. At the sacred table, it is there; in the ordination of priests, it is there; in the mystical Supper of the Saviour, it is there. It is drawn on every point of the horizon, on the tops of houses, over public places, in inhabited parts and in deserts, on roads, on mountains, in woods, on hills, on the sea, on the masts of ships, on islands, on windows, over doors, on the necks of Christians, on beds, garments, books, arms, and banquet-couches, in feasts, on gold and silver vessels, on precious stones, on the pictures of the apartments.

"It is made over sick animals, over those possessed by the demon, in war, in peace, by day, by night, in pleasant reunions, and in penitential assemblies. It is an honorable contest as to who shall seek first the protection of this admirable sign.

"What is there surprising in this? The Sign of the Cross is the type of our deliverance, the monument of the liberation of mankind, the *souvenir* of the forbearance of Our Lord. When you make it, remember what has been given for your ransom, and you will be the slave of no one. Make it then not only with your fingers, but with your faith. If you thus engrave it on your forehead, no impure spirit shall dare to stand before you. He sees the cutlass with which he has been wounded, the sword from which he has received his death-blow. If at the sight of patibulary places (places of execution) we are seized with horror, think what satan and his angels must suffer at the sight of that weapon which was used by the Eternal Word to weaken their power, and strike off the head of the dragon." [Quod Christus sit Deus, app. t. i. p. 697, edit. Paris altera; id in Matth. homil. 54. app. t. vii. p. 620, et in c. iii. ad Phillip.]

To-morrow, I will discuss the reflections produced by this ravishing spectacle, so eloquently described.

Mgr. J. J. Gaume

Seventeenth Letter

Summary—Nature of the Sign of the Cross—How it is valued at the present day—What the contempt and forgetfulness of the Sign of the Cross announce—Spectacle of the present world—satan returns—To remain faithful to the Sign of the Cross—Principally before and after meals—Reason, honor, and liberty command it—Is reason for or against those who make the Sign of the Cross over food?—Examples and arguments

December 12th

My Dear Frederic,

A universal weapon, an invincible weapon for man, lightning-conductor for creatures, souvenir of man's deliverance, and trophy of victory for the Word Redeemer:— such, my dear Frederic, was the Sign of the Cross in the eyes of the first Christians. Thence came the use they made of it, the sentiments with which it inspired them, and the magnificent spectacle we have just witnessed. Have we retained the faith of our forefathers? What is the Sign of the Cross to the Christians of the nineteenth century? What use do they make of it, either for themselves or for creatures? Are the sentiments of faith, confidence, respect, gratitude and love which it awakens in them, lively, or even real? And among those who do make it, do not the greater part make it without knowing what they are doing, without attaching to it either any great value, or any considerable importance? How many are there who no longer make it? How many who are ashamed to do so? How many, even, who do not like to see it made? They have removed it from the tops of their houses, banished it out of their apartments, and effaced it from their furniture. They have caused it to disappear from the public places and walks of their cities; from the gardens and parks of their villas; from the roads of their villages; from the greater part of the places in which our forefathers erected it. They have broken the crosses!

What means this? What do such symptoms announce? Do you wish to know? Reascend to that principle which throws light on all history. Two contrary spirits dispute between them the empire of the world; the spirit of good, and the spirit of evil. All that is done, is by divine inspiration or by satanic inspiration. The institution of the Sign of the Cross, the incessant use of the Sign of the Cross, the confidence in the Sign of the Cross, the omnipotent virtue attributed to the Sign of the Cross—are they the result of a divine or a satanic inspiration? It must be either one or the other. If of satanic inspiration, then the élite of humanity, who alone make the Sign of the Cross, have for more than eighteen centuries been struck with incurable blindness, while all those who do not belong to the élite of humanity have been in full possession of the light; this would be to say that the near-sighted, those blind of an eye or totally blind, see more clearly than those who have two good eyes. Do you think there is a pride so desperate as to advance such a paradox, an incredulity so strong as to sustain it? But if it is by divine inspiration that the Sign of the Cross is practiced, repeated, cherished and regarded as the invincible, universal, permanent, and necessary weapon of mankind, what shall we think of a world that no longer understands the Sign of the Cross, that no longer makes it, that despises it, is ashamed of it, no longer salutes it, wishes it no longer in its sight, or under the face of its sun?

Unless human nature is radically changed, and dualism but a chimera; unless satan has withdrawn from the combat; unless creatures have ceased to be the medium of his fatal influence, the Christian of to-day, the despiser of the Sign of the Cross, is but an unworthy scion of a noble race. The nineteenth century is a foolish rationalist, who understands neither the combat, nor the conditions of the combat; a presumptuous soldier, who, after having broken his weapon and thrown aside his armor, casts himself blindly, with his arms bound and his breast bared, into the midst of swords and lances; modern society is a dismantled city, surrounded by innumerable enemies, impatient to reduce it to ruins, and put the garrison to the sword.

To reduce it to ruins? But is it not already a ruin? A ruin of belief, ruin of morals, ruin of authority, ruin of tradition, ruin of the fear of God and of conscience, ruin of virtue, probity, mortification, obedience, the spirit of sacrifice, resignation, and hope—on all sides, ruin either commenced or consummated.

In public and in private life, in city and in country, in him who governs, and those who are governed, in the order of ideas and the dominion of facts, how many men or things remain truly and sincerely Catholic?

In this, dear Frederic, there is nothing that ought to astonish us. Take away the Sign of the Cross, and all shall be explained. The less of the Sign of the Cross in the world, the more of satan. The Sign of the Cross is the lightning-rod of the world; remove it, and the thunderbolt falls which shall burn and crush you.

The Sign of the Cross is a trophy which attests the dominion of the victor. To break it, is to give joy to the ancient enemy of mankind, and prepare the way for his return. Listen to what was written seventeen centuries ago by one of those men who best understood the mysterious power of the Sign of the Cross. I mean that martyr, illustrious among all others, St. Ignatius, of Antioch. Contemplate that white-haired bishop, loaded with chains, traveling four hundred leagues to be devoured by lions under the eyes of the great city of Rome. See him, as calm as if standing at the altar, as joyful as if going to a feast; sowing, on his way, instruction and encouragement to the churches of Asia, which hasten to meet him in his passage. In his admirable letter to the Christians of Philippi, he says: "The prince of this world rejoices when he sees any one abandon the Cross. He knows it is the Cross that brings death to him, for it is the weapon destructive to his power. The sight of it horrifies him, the name frightens him. Before it was made, he neglected no means of having it constructed, and to this work he incited the children of unbelief, Judas, the Pharisees, the Sadducees, the old, the young, and the priests. But when he saw it on the point of being completed, he was troubled. He excited remorse in the soul of the traitor, presented him with the rope, and tempted him to hang himself. He troubled Pilate's wife by a painful dream, and made every effort to prevent the construction of the Cross. Not because he had remorse; if he had felt it, he would not have been wholly bad; but he had a presentiment of his defeat. He was not deceived. The Cross is the principle of his condemnation, the principle of his death, the principle of his ruin."

Thence come two teachings; horror and fear of the demon at the sight of the Cross and the Sign of the Cross; and his joy at the absence of both one and the other. If he sees a soul or a country without the Sign of the Cross, he enters it fearlessly, and remains there at his ease. As inevitably as darkness succeeds light after the setting of the sun, so inevitably does he there re-establish his empire. The present world is a sensible proof of it.

I do not speak of that deluge of denials, impieties, and unheard-of blasphemies with which it is inundated. What are (for those who are not satisfied with words) those millions of table-turnings, those spirit-rappings or familiar spirits, those apparitions, incantations, oracles, medical consultations, and pretended conversations with the dead, which have so suddenly invaded the old and new world?*

Are these things new? No; mankind has already seen them. At what epoch? When the Sign of the Cross did not protect mankind, and satan was the king, the god of society. By reappearing to-day in a degree unknown since ancient paganism, what do they signify, if not that the Sign of the Cross ceasing now to protect the world, satan is retaking possession of it.

You see, dear friend, how little intelligence have those who abandon the Sign of the Cross. Let us pity, but not imitate them.

There is one circumstance, in particular, in which we must invariably separate ourselves from them. With us, as with our forefathers, the Sign of the Cross before and after meals must be a sacred duty. Reason, honor, and liberty demand it.

---

* At the time in which we are writing there is an unparalleled recrudescence of occult practices. In Paris, Spiritualism has formed numerous associations, which have their regular meetings. Besides many books, they have three special papers to serve as their periodical organs. Metz and Bordeaux, you may be sure, contain many thousand Spiritualists. In Lyons there are at least fifteen thousand, with a journal, in which they pretend that the religion of Spirit-rapping is to be the religion of the future. What does all this mean? Simply, that after eighteen centuries of Christianity, there are in France thousands of idolaters, who either ignorantly or designedly do what was done two thousand years ago at Delphi, at Dodona, at Sinope, and all the cities of pagan antiquity. Things have arrived to such a state that many bishops have been obliged to warn the clergy and faithful of their dioceses against the usurpation of satan.

Reason. If you ask your companions why they do not make the Sign of the Cross before taking food, each will answer: "I do not wish to make myself singular by doing differently from others: I do not wish to be remarked and laughed at for observing a useless and obsolete practice." They do not wish to make themselves singular? For the sake of their honor, I will believe that they do not understand the import of these words. To be singular, is to put one's self in the singular number, to isolate one's self, and to act differently from everybody else. In this sense we may very well be singular without being ridiculous. One is sometimes obliged to be so, under pain of being guilty. A reasonable man, who, in a mad-house, performs sensible actions; an honest man, who, in a land of thieves, respects the property of others, are both singular — are they ridiculous? To be singular, in the sense in which your companions understand it, is to differ ridiculously from established usages. It remains to be seen, whether by making the Sign of the Cross before and after meals, we make ourselves singular, and this in a ridiculous manner. "Without doubt," answer they, "since you act differently from others."

But there are *others* and *others*. There are *others* who make the Sign of the Cross; and *others* who do *not* make it. Therefore by making it we are no more singular than by not making it, we remain perfectly in the plural. Are we ridiculous? To answer this, it suffices to see who are the *others* who make, and the *others* who do not make the Sign of the Cross.

The *others* who make it, are you and I, your respected family and mine; and we are not alone. Behind us, around us, beside us, are the true, learned and courageous Catholics who have lived in the East and West during eighteen centuries. Now, as we have seen, those Catholics, neither more nor less, have formed the élite of mankind. We are so far from being ridiculous by remaining in such company, that we become perfectly so by separating ourselves from them. Except for those who are satisfied with words, and who would wish to satisfy others with the same, this proposition is indisputable.

Nothing is more fully established than that the élite of mankind have always made the Sign of the Cross before meals. The Fathers whom I have quoted, Tertullian, St. Cyril, St. Ephrem, and St. John Chrysostom, leave us no doubt as to the universality of this religious practice among the Christians of the primitive Church. To these, I will add a few others.

"When," says St. Athanasius, "we sit down to table, and take the bread to break it, we make the Sign of the Cross over it three times, and return thanks. After the repast, we renew our thanksgiving by saying thrice: 'The good and merciful Lord has given food to those that fear Him. Glory be to the Father, etc.' " [De Virginit., n. 13.]

And St. Jerome: "Let no one ever sit at table without having prayed, and let him never leave it without giving thanks to the Creator." [Epist. xxii. ad Eustoch., *De Custod. Virginit.*]

St. Chrysostom brands as they deserve, those who dispense themselves from this sacred law of wisdom and gratitude. "We must pray before and after meals. Hear this, ye swine who nourish yourselves with the gifts of God, without raising your eyes to the hand that gives them." [Homil. 82, in Matth., n. 2. t. vii., p. 885; id Homil. 49, in id. n. 2. p. 569, edit. novi.]

The blessing of the table by the Sign of the Cross was in use not only in families and in private life; the soldiers in their camps observed it with religious fidelity. On this point, St. Gregory of Nazianzen relates a fact which is still famous.

Julian the Apostate was rewarding his troops by an

extraordinary distribution of money and provisions. Near the emperor was placed a lighted perfume pan, into which each soldier cast a few grains of incense. The Christian soldiers did like the others, never suspecting that by it they rendered themselves guilty of an act of idolatry. The distribution being over, the soldiers reassembled for the feast of the prince. At the beginning of the banquet the cup was presented to a Christian soldier, who, according to custom, blessed it by the Sign of the Cross. Suddenly a voice was heard, saying: "What you are now doing is in contradiction to what you have just done." "What have I done?" "Have you, then, forgotten the incense and the perfume pan? Do you not know that you have performed an act of idolatry, and denied your faith?" At these words he and his brave companions-in-arms arose from the table, and sighing, groaning and tearing their hair, they rushed out, declaring aloud that they were Christians, accusing the emperor of having deceived them, and demanding another trial, that they might confess their faith. The Apostate ordered them to be arrested, bound, condemned, and led to the place of execution. But not wishing to make them martyrs, he commuted the sentence of death into that of exile to the farthest parts of the empire. [Orat. I. Contr. Julian; Theodoret, Hist., lib. iii. c. 16.]

Whenever a priest was among the guests, on him was conferred the honor of making the Sign of the Cross over the food. [See D. Ruinart, Acts of the Martyrdom of S. Theodota.]

The blessing at table was regarded so holy a practice, that in the ninth century we find the Bulgarians converted to the faith, asking Pope Nicholas I., if a layman might take the place of a priest in performing this function. "Without doubt," answered the pope, "for it has been given to each one to preserve by the Sign of the Cross all that belongs to him from the snares of the demon, and in the name of Our Lord Jesus Christ, to triumph over his attacks." [Rep. ad consult. Bulgar.]

Succeeding ages have seen the use of the Sign of the Cross before and after meals, among the true Catholics of the East and West; you know that it still exists.

We know the *others* that make the Sign of the Cross before meals. Let us see who are the *others* that do *not* make it, and to whom your young companions give the preference.

Pagans do not make it; Jews do not make it; heretics do not make it; atheists do not make it; bad Catholics do not make it; ignorant Catholics, or those enslaved by human respect, do not make it. Behold those *others* who do not make the Sign of the Cross, and who laugh at those who do: on which side is the ridiculous singularity?

In my next letter I shall follow up this objection.

Mgr. J.J.Gaume

Eighteenth Letter

Honor commands us to pray before and after meals — Prayer over food is as ancient as the world, as wide-spread as the human race — Proofs: *Benedicite* and *Grace* of every people — Not to say them is to liken ourselves to beings which do not belong to the human species — The blessing at table is a law of humanity

December 13th

My Dear Friend,

Honor is a second motive for remaining faithful to the ancient custom of making the Sign of the Cross before and after meals. Your companions, on the contrary, seem to think it honorable to abstain from it. They say: "I do not wish to be remarked and laughed at." Let us pass to the examination of this new pretext.

First: reason, as we have seen, condemns the scorners of the Sign of the Cross, consequently honor cannot absolve them. Honor is never on the side of unreasonableness. They add that they do not wish to be remarked. Impossible! whatever they do, they are remarked. I do not believe them so unfortunate as never to find themselves at table with true Catholics. But then they make themselves necessarily remarked, and very sadly, I assure you.

It is true, since they say it, that this is a matter of indifference to them. Is this haughty disdain well-founded? Here recurs the question already resolved of *others* and *others*. As to the mockery of which they are afraid, it follows the remark. Only with the true Catholic it is turned into pity. Nevertheless, in contenting myself with exposing your companions and their fellows to the remarks of Catholics, I have been indulgent. You shall see that in abstaining from prayer before taking their meals, under pretext of not making themselves remarkable, they disgrace themselves before all mankind. Follow me. He who disgraces himself in the sight of every one, is the man who voluntarily places himself in the rank of beasts.

Until now, there was but one class of beings that ate without praying. Now we know of two—beasts, and those that resemble them. I say *that resemble them*, for between a dog, and a man that eats without praying, what is the difference? As for me, I see none; neither does the Academy of Science.

A biped or a quadruped, sitting or lying, murmuring, chattering, or growling, they have, one as well as the other, hands or paws, eyes, heart and teeth sunk into matter, stupidly devouring their food without raising their heads toward the hand that gives it. The man, who acts thus, degrades himself from the class of human beings; as a beast, he sits at table, a beast, he remains there, a beast, he leaves it.

My propositions seem to you too absolute, and you exclaim: "Is it really true, as you say, that before our time there were known only beasts, oxen, asses, mules, swine, oysters, crocodiles, that ate without praying?"

Nothing is more certain. PRAYER OVER FOOD IS AS ANCIENT AS THE WORLD; AS WIDE-SPREAD AS MANKIND.

From all antiquity we find it among the Jews. "When thou hast eaten, and art full," says the Mosaic law, "bless the Lord." [Deut. viii. 10.] Behold prayer over food. Faithful to this divine ordinance, the Jews, while eating, observed the following ceremonies. The father of the family, surrounded by his children, said:

"Blessed be the Lord our God, whose goodness gives food to all flesh." Then taking a cup of wine in his right hand, he blessed it, saying: "Blessed be the Lord our God, who has created the fruit of the vine." He first tasted it, and then passed it to his guests, who also tasted it. Then followed the blessing of the bread. Taking it all between his hands, the father of the family said: "Praised and blessed be the Lord our God, who has drawn bread from the earth." He then broke the bread, ate a piece, and gave some to his guests. It was only then that the meal began. When they changed the wine or brought in new dishes, a particular blessing was made over each, so that every kind of nourishment was purified and consecrated. The meal being ended, they sang a hymn of thanksgiving. [Stuckius, Antiq. convivial., lib. ii., c. 36. p. 436. ed. in folio, 1695.]

All these rites are so much the more venerable, as they have been consecrated by the Son of God Himself. Nothing could more clearly prove their importance. What did the adorable Teacher of mankind at His last Supper, when he ate the Paschal Lamb with His disciples? What did He, when, after Supper, He sang with them a hymn of thanksgiving? *Et hymno dicto exierunt in montem Oliveti* (And a hymn being said, they went out unto mount Olivet). [St. Matthew 26:30] He religiously conformed Himself to the usages of the holy nation. He took the cup, blessed it, and passed it to each of the guests. [St. Luke xxii. 17.]

In how many other cases do we see the Eternal Model of man, praying before taking or giving food! He breaks the bread, divides the fishes, and distributes them among the people. Having taken the five loaves and two fishes, He raised His eyes to heaven and blessed them. [St. Mark viii. St. Matth. xiv.]

All these expressions, according to the Fathers, show the blessing of the food. The Incarnate Word made it in order to teach us never to eat without the blessing and thanksgiving. [Theophylact, in Matth. xiv.] Is it then surprising that we find the blessing at table in use among the first Christians? Were not the examples of the Man-God the rule of their conduct? Did the apostles do anything else but recollect them constantly?

"With us," says Polydore Vergil, "the custom is to bless the table before meals; this is done in imitation of Our Lord. The Gospel relates that He conformed Himself to this custom, when in the desert He blessed the five loaves, and at Emmaus, the table of the two disciples." [Apud Stuckius, p. 428.]

Tertullian says: "Prayer begins and ends the meal." [Apol. iii. 9.]

I might also quote St. Chrysostom, St. Jerome, Origen, both the Latin and Greek Fathers; [See Duranti, *De ritibus* Eccl. Cath. lib. ii. p. 658. Edit. 1592.] but the fact not being disputed, why should I multiply testimonies? I will only add, that we have the *Benedicite* and *Grace* of the first Christians in the magnificent verses of Prudentius: *Christi prius Genitore potens, etc.* (The first glory to the Father of Christ).

These hymns are another proof of the exactitude with which our ancestors conformed themselves to the example of Our Lord, as He Himself conformed to the usage of the ancient Jews, and they to the command of God Himself.

We have them also in prose. See these monuments of our thrice venerable antiquity.

Before meals: "O Thou who givest food to all that breathe, deign to bless the food we are about to take. Thou hast said that if we should ever drink any poisonous thing, we should receive no injury thereby, provided we would invoke Thy name, for Thou art all-powerful. Take away, then, from this food all that is dangerous and hurtful in it." [See Mamachi: Customs of Primitive Christians, t. ii. p. 47, Origen., in Joan, p. 36.]

After meals: "Blessed be Thou, O Lord our God, who hast nourished us since our infancy, and with us all that breathe.

Fill our hearts with joy, that we may abound in all kinds of good works, through Jesus Christ our Lord, to whom, with Thee and the Holy Ghost, be glory, honor and power. Amen." [Stuckius, *ubi supra.* p. 129.]

These formulas, so profoundly philosophical, as we shall soon see, have been handed down for ages. Whether modified or not, they have remained in use to our time. Notwithstanding their hostility to the Church, many Protestants have retained them.

Even to this day, a great many families in Germany and England never take their meals without praying. What will appear still stranger to you, is that the blessing of the table is found among pagan nations. Yes, my dear Frederic, the Romans and Greeks, those obliging models of our college youth, made religiously that which your companions, their disciples and admirers, are ashamed to do. "Never did the ancients," says Athenæus, "take their meals without having first implored their gods." [Dipnosophis, lib. iv.]

Speaking of the Egyptians in particular, he adds: "Having taken their places on the banquet-couches, they arose, knelt down, and the chief of the banquet or the priest began the traditional prayers, which they recited after him; after that they resumed their places." [Ibid. lib. iv.]

The same thing among the Romans. Speaking of an order for the assassination of a man, given by Consul Quintius Flaminius during a banquet to please a courtesan, Titus Livy thus expresses himself: "This monstrous act was committed in the midst of vessels filled with wine; in the midst of a repast, when it is the custom to pray to the gods, and offer libations." [Decad. iv. lib. ix.]

You are aware that those libations were a form of prayer,

known everywhere and very frequently repeated. The Romans, for example, made them at almost every hour of the day; when they arose in the morning; when they retired at night; when going on a journey; in the sacrifices, at marriages, at the beginning and end of meals. Those ancient masters of the world never touched food until they had consecrated a part to their divinities. The portion thus retrenched from the banquet was placed on an altar, or a *patella* (vase), which took the place of it. This was their *Benedicite* and their *Grace*.

Remarkable perpetuity of tradition! We have seen that among the Jews, the blessing was renewed at the changing of the wine, and at each new dish. The same was the custom of the Romans. At the second course there were particular libations to the gods whom they believed to preside at table. Each guest poured out on the table or the floor, a little of the wine in the cup, and recited certain prayers to the gods. [Dict. of Antiq, art. Libations.]

The Greeks had served as models to the Romans. Among them are found the same frequency and the same custom of libations at the beginning and end of the meal; the same particular prayers at changing the wine. "Each time," says Diodorus of Sicily, "that they gave pure wine to the guests, the ancient custom was to say: 'The gift of the good Spirit;' and when, at the end of the meal, they gave wine mixed with water, they said: 'The Gift of Jupiter Saviour,' because pure wine is as contrary to the health of the soul as to that of the body." [Lib. iv.]

They were not satisfied with particular *Grace*: they had also a general one, which ended the meal in which *Jovis servatoris*, (they addressed Jupiter). [Id. lib. ii.]

The custom of blessing the food was so much respected,

among the Pagans, that it gave rise to the following proverb: "*Ne a chytropode cibum nondum sanctificatum* rapias (Do not draw out of the cauldron the nonsanctified food)."

"This proverb," says Erasmus, "signifies, Do not throw yourself on food, like a beast, and eat only after having offered the first fruits to the gods." In fact, among the ancients, according to Plutarch, the repasts, even daily ones, were reckoned among the number of sacred things. For this reason the guests consecrated the first part to the gods, testifying by their deportment, that the act of eating was for them a mysterious and holy thing. [Apud. Stuckius, p. 431.]

Again at the celebrated banquet of the suburbs of Antioch, Julian the Apostate, in order to renew publicly the chain of pagan tradition, took care to have the tables blessed by a priest of Apollo. [Sozomen. Hist. lib. 3. c. 4.] In this, the barbarians imitated civilized nations. During their meals, the Vandals handed around a cup consecrated to their gods by certain formulas. [Crantz, lib. iii. Vandal., c. 37.]

In India the king never tasted any dish which had not first been consecrated to the demon.

Notwithstanding the difference of manners, civilization and climate, the inhabitants of the Frigid zone had the same practice as those of the Torrid. The ancient Lithuanians, Samogitians, and other northern barbarians, called on the demons to sanctify their tables, and they came. In a corner of their huts they kept familiar serpents. On certain days they caused them to go up on the table by means of a white table cloth: they tasted of every dish, and then returned to their holes. The meats were considered sanctified, and the barbarians ate of them without any fear. [Stuckius, p. 431.]

The blessing of the table is equally found among the Turks

and modern Jews. Faithful to the traditions of their ancestors, the latter even preserve the custom of saying many prayers during meals.

Thus, when they bring fruits they say: "Blessed be the Lord our God, who has created the fruit of the trees." At dessert: "Blessed be the Lord our God, who has created different kinds of food." [Stuckius, *ubi supra*; et c. xxxviii. *Delibationibus ante et post epulas.*]

Gross as their customs are, the people of Chin-India, of China and Thibet, are no exception to the general custom, which I am confident might be found to exist even among the degraded negroes of Africa.

"We arrived at the great pagoda of Ouen-chou-yuen, a little before eleven o'clock," writes a missionary in China. "It was just the time when the bonzes sat down to table. Behold the spectacle of which we became the witnesses. In a vast refectory, ninety bonzes were seated back to back, before a long and very narrow table; with their hands joined, their eyes constantly fixed on the floor, they sang together some words which none of us could understand. This prayer lasted more than ten minutes. The chief bonze was in the centre behind a gilded idol, praying and sitting like the others, but alone before a small table, somewhat raised above the others, on a platform, whence he had a view of the whole assembly. In the middle of the refectory, and facing the idol, was another bonze dressed in yellow, who offered to the god a bowl of rice. Prayer being ended, he who offered the rice placed it under the chin of the god. Then the servants hastened to fill the dishes on the different tables. None of the guests moved. The chief bonze gave the signal, and all fell to work. In an instant they had devoured a large number of buckets of rice, in true tavern fashion, and that was all." [Annals of Prop. of Faith, n. 95, p. 340, A. D.

Behold the *Benedicite* in its most solemn form. In this manner was it said by the first Christians; in this manner is it still said in seminaries and religious communities:—what a clever ape satan is!

As I have already said, you see, dear friend, that prayer before and after meals is as ancient as the world, as wide-spread as the human race. If then, the existence of a law is recognized by the permanency of its effects; if, for example, a man, by seeing the sun rise every morning at a particular point of the horizon, is warranted in saying that a law regulates its movements;— have I then, less reason to affirm that the blessing of the food is a law of humanity? To observe it, is to do like the rest of mankind. Not to observe it, is to act like beasts, which do not belong to the human species. It is literally to liken one's self to a beast. [Ps. 48.]

You may ask your companions if honor here finds its reckoning. We shall soon come to the explanation of that law which commands the blessing of the table.

Mgr. J. J. Gaume

Nineteenth Letter

Reasons for the blessing of the table—It is an act of freedom—
Three tyrants; the world, the flesh, the devil—Triple victory of the
Sign of the Cross and prayer over food—Victory over the world:
proofs—Over the flesh: proofs—Over the demon: proofs—
Remarkable testimony of Porphyrius—Facts cited by St. Gregory—
Conclusion

December 15th

My Dear Frederic,

"It is only crocodiles that eat without praying." Such, you
will say to me, dear friend, is the axiom which summed up
your last letter.

Your words shall remain.

"My comrades," you add, "have been *beaten down*, as you
say in France, by the facts that you have related, facts perfectly
new to them. Notwithstanding all this, they do not, to-day any
more than yesterday, make the Sign of the Cross before and
after their meals. The only difference is, that I may make it
with impunity: they are afraid of my axiom."

These details do not surprise me. Your companions and
their associates, like many other great talkers about liberty and
independence, are slaves—slaves of the vilest of tyrants,
human respect. Poor young men! In order to conceal their
slavery, they end their objections by saying: "The Sign of the
Cross is a useless and obsolete practice." In their intimate
thoughts, this language signifies:

"All those who do not eat as we do, that is, like beasts,
belong to a more or less respectable species of blockheads;
priests and religious are blockheads; true Catholics of every
nation, blockheads; the Jews, Egyptians, Greeks, Romans,
blockheads; the élite of humanity, blockheads; the whole of

humanity; blockheads; my father, mother, sisters, all are blockheads. I, and those like me, are the only wise ones on earth, the only enlightened ones among mortals."

I must then tear off the mask with which they try to cover themselves. For this, it suffices to show that the blessing at table with the Sign of the Cross is an act of freedom, an act very useful, an act out of fashion only in the lowest ranks of modern Christianity. Joined to reason and honor, this last consideration fully justifies our conduct, at the same time that it gives an account of the universal practice of mankind.

Freedom

Three tyrants dispute the liberty of man; yours and mine as well as that of your companions. Those tyrants are the world, the flesh, and the devil. It is in order that we be not enslaved by any of them, that we, and all mankind with us, make use of the blessing of the table. We have seen, and I repeat it, that not to make the Sign of the Cross before we eat, is to separate ourselves from the élite of mankind; not to pray, is to liken ourselves to beasts. In either case it is to be slaves.

Submission to despotic power is what constitutes slavery. Despotic power is that which has no right to command, or which commands against reason, against justice, against authority. What, then, is that power which prevents me from making the Sign of the Cross before my meals; and, if I be so courageous as to disobey, threatens me with its scorn? What authority has it? From whom does it hold its commission? And what are the titles which recommend it to my obedience, the reasons which justify its prohibition? This usurping power is the world of the present day: a world unknown in the annals of Christian ages, the world of drawing-rooms, theatres, cafés, hotels, stock-jobbing and exchange; it is the customs of this world, the impiety of this world, the gross materialism of this world, the Bœotia of the intellect. Now this minority, born yesterday and already decrepit; this factious minority, in continual insurrection against reason, honor and mankind, has the insolence to impose its caprices on me! And shall I be base enough to submit? And after having taken my divorce from reason, honor, and the élite of mankind, shall I dare to speak of liberty, dignity, and independence? Vain parade! Beneath the gilded tinsel of pride would pierce the chains of slavery; my tattered disguise would but poorly conceal the figure of the beast, and good sense would follow me, repeating: "Midas, King Midas has ass' ears." Let the independents of our day be flattered by such a compliment; it is their own affair. As for us blockheads, we do not want it at any price. Shameful is the slavery of the world; more shameful that of vice. Ingratitude is a vice, gluttony is a vice, impurity is a vice. Against these tyrants we are protected by the Sign of the Cross, and prayer before and after meals.

Ingratitude

There are at the present day two religions: that of respect, and that of contempt. The first respects God, the Church, authority, tradition, the soul, the body, and creatures. To it, all is sacred, because all comes from God, all belongs to God, all must return to God. It teaches me to use everything in the spirit of dependence, because nothing is mine; in the spirit of fear, because I shall have to render an account of all; in the spirit of gratitude, because everything is a benefit, even the air I breathe.

The second despises everything; God, the Church, authority, tradition, the soul, the body, and creatures. Its sectaries use and abuse life and the gifts of God, as if they were the proprietors of them, and proprietors wholly irresponsible. The first has inscribed on its banner the word "Gratitude;" the second, "Ingratitude." Both one and the other show themselves at the moment in which man, by manducation (eating), assimilates to himself the divine gifts necessary for life. Faithful to the religion of respect, the élite of humanity pray and return thanks. They have too keen a sense of their dignity to confound themselves with beasts; too lively a sense of duty to remain mute when they see themselves loaded with so many gifts. If ingratitude in regard to man be odious, they, with good reason, find it a thousand times more so in regard to God.

To be the slaves of such a vice is a disgrace which they cannot endure. Shame on him for whom gratitude is a burden too heavy to bear; the ungrateful heart was never a good heart. An adept in the religion of contempt is ashamed of gratitude. He eats like the beast, or like an unnatural son, who has neither in his heart a sentiment of tenderness, nor on his lips an expression of gratitude for the father whose inexhaustible goodness provides for all his wants, and even for his pleasures.

"Do you see that child, so tenderly raised," says an illustrious Chancellor of England, "him, who, seated at his father's table, eats his bread without ever speaking of him; often outrages him by words, and who, as soon as filled, turns his back on him as on a stranger to whom he owes nothing?" [Th. Morus, ap Duranti, De ritibus, etc. lib. ii. p. 659.] And because he exempts himself from duty, he believes himself to be free! He proclaims himself independent! Independent of whom, and of what? Independent of all that should be hated and despised. A glorious independence, truly!

Gluttony

Another tyrant, who seated at table with us, and by the viands, captivating the sight, taste and smell, prostrates man in adoration before the god of the belly. His mouth, instead of speaking from the abundance of the heart, speaks only of his stomach. It is the taste of food which he seeks, and not its repairing quality. He does not eat that he may live; he lives that he may eat. In the meantime, organism develops its empire; the intellect is darkened, the soul becomes enslaved. Good cheer is incompatible with wisdom. A great man was never a glutton; all the saints have been models of sobriety. [Job xxviii. 13.]

Take notice, dear friend, that I speak only of the gluttony which seeks rich food, of delicacy in the choice, and greediness and sensuality in eating. Too frequently it is followed by intemperance. Now intemperance is attended by such a train of infirmities and diseases, that *plures accidit crapula quam gladius* (gluttony kills more men than the sword)." [Eccles. 31:23; 37:34.]

Therefore Nebuchadnezzar, Pharaoh, Alexander, Cæsar, Tamerlane, and all those crowned persecutors who covered the world with dead bodies, have caused the death of fewer men than has gluttony. Frightful mystery, which shows what profound wisdom there is in the Sign of the Cross and prayer before and after meals! By these we call God to our help, and arm ourselves against a perfidious enemy, which attacks all ages, sexes, and conditions, and which tends to enslave us to the grossest instincts. By them we learn that eating is a warfare, and that, in order not to be vanquished, we must, according to the words of a great genius, take our food as we take remedies, through necessity, and not for pleasure. [S. Aug. Confess., lib. x. c. 31.]

Impurity

Commenced by gluttony, the slavery of the soul ends by impurity.—Whoever feeds his flesh with delicacies, shall suffer its most shameful revolt.—The fat and plump slave will resist.—Wine is a luxurious beverage.—In wine is luxury. [Luxuriosa res vinum, Prov. xx. i.]—Pure wine is as contrary to the health of the soul as to that of the body.—Drunk inconsiderately, it foams voluptuousness.—In the stomach of a young man, wine is oil to the fire.

—Gluttony is the mother of luxury, the executioner of chastity.—To be greedy, yet expect to be chaste, is to wish to quench a fire with oil.—Gluttony is the extinguisher of the intellect.—The glutton is an idolater; he adores the god of the belly. The temple of this god is the kitchen; his altar, the table; his priests, the cooks; his victim, the dishes; his incense, the odor of the viands.—This temple is the school of impurity.— Bacchus and Venus go hand in hand.—Gluttony always attacks us; if it triumph, it immediately calls in its sister Luxury.— Gluttony and Luxury are two inseparable demons.

—A multitude of dishes and bottles draws a multitude of impure spirits: the worse of all is the demon of the belly.—The physical and moral health of the people may be judged by the number of cooks.*

You have heard the oracles of divine and profane wisdom. It is the voice of ages confirmed by experience. What means has man for preserving his liberty in the face of an enemy, so much the more dangerous, because he binds and kills while he flatters? The past and present know only one; it is the help of God. The future shall know no other.

The help of God is obtained by prayer. One special prayer has been established and practiced among all nations, to fortify man against the temptations of the table. Those who make it are not always victorious. [S. Aug., Confess. lib. x. 31.] And those who never make it, who despise it, who scoff at it, would wish to persuade us that they always remain masters of the battle-field. In order to believe them, it is necessary to have other proof than words; we must have facts. These facts are their morals. Let them, then, bring to light the mysteries of their thoughts, their desires, their looks, their private discourses,

---

* Gula genitrix est luxuriæ et castitatis carnifex. (S. Hier., Regul. monach., c. xxxv.) Qui ventri diem obsequitur, fornicationis spiritum vincere vult, is ei similis est, qui oleo incendium extinguere nititur. (S. Joan. Clim., Grad., xiv.)—Deo ventri templum, est coquina; altare, mensa; ministri, coqui, immolatæ pecudes, coctæ carnes; fumus incensorum, odor saporum. (Hug. a. S. Vict., De claustr. anim., lib. ii. c. 19.) Esus carnium et potus vini, ventrisque saturitas, seminarium libidinus est: unde comicus, sine Cerere, iniquit, et Libero friget Venus. (S. Hier., ad Jovin., lib. ii.) Immundi spiritus se moegis injiciunt, ubi plus viderint escarum et potuum. (S. Isidor. Hisp., De sum. bono, c. xliv. sent. 3.)—Gula et Luxuria, conjurata dæmoniæ. (Tertull.)—Multos morbos, multa fercula ferunt: innumerabiles esse morbos miraris? coquos numera.—(Seneca, Ep. xcv. etc. etc.)

their conduct. But such a revelation is not necessary; we have it every week in the gazettes of scandal and public immorality.

The demon. It is here that the stupid ignorance of the present world shows itself most plainly. Without doubt the sacred duty of gratitude, as well as the imperative necessity of defending ourselves against gluttony and voluptuousness, fully justifies the usage of the blessing at table. I dare affirm, however, that there remains a reason more profound and more powerful. We have said it; there is a dogma of which mankind has never lost the remembrance; that of the subjection of all creatures to the prince of evil since his victory over the father of our race.

All nations have believed, as much as in the existence of God, that creatures penetrated by the malignant influences of the demon, become the instruments of his hatred against man. Thence the infinite variety of purifications employed in all religions, all ages, and all climates. But there is one circumstance in which the use of those purifications is invariably shown; it is in the act of manducation. The universality and invariability of this custom at meal time is founded on two facts. The first, that the demon of the table is the most dangerous; [Clem. Alex. Poedag., lib. ii. c. i.] the second, that the union operated by manducation between man and his food is most intimate, reaching even to assimilation. Of the food that he has digested, man may say: "It is bone of my bone, flesh of my flesh, blood of my blood."

Behold why, creatures being vitiated, God has never permitted that man should lose sight of the extreme danger of communication with them. That this universal fear is a deep reason of the existence of the Sign of the Cross and of prayer over food, is proved even by the formulas of blessing and thanksgiving. Christians or pagans, all without exception, ask the removal of the malevolent influences with which creatures are filled.

Do you wish for something stronger, something that may be more convincing to your companions than all the authorities drawn from the Church? Porphyrius, the greatest theologian of paganism, the most learned interpreter of the rites and mysteries of ancient idolatry, says in characteristic terms:

"It must be known that the dwellings are full of demons. This is why we purify them by expelling those malevolent hosts, every time we pray to the gods. Moreover, all creatures are full of them, for they particularly relish certain kinds of food. So *when we sit at table, they not only place themselves beside us, but also attach themselves to our bodies.* Thence comes the use of lustrations (purifying by sacrifice or washing), the principal end of which is not so much to invoke the gods as to expel the demons. They take delight principally in blood and impurities, and in order to satisfy themselves, enter into the bodies of those who are subject to them. There is no violent motion in the flesh, no vehement desire of lust in the spirit, which is not excited by the presence of those hosts." [Apud Euseb. Præp. evang. lib. iv. c. 22.]

Is it St. Paul whom we have just heard? We might believe it, so precise is this revelation of the mysteries of the supernatural world. Besides the occult and permanent influences of the demons over our food, God permits, from time to time, striking facts, which reveal the presence of the enemy, and the necessity of banishing him before making use of them. We read the following in St. Gregory the Great:

"In the monastery of the abbot Equitius, it happened that a religious, going one day into the garden, saw a lettuce which excited her appetite. She took it, and forgetting to make the Sign of the Cross, ate it with avidity. At the same instant she was possessed by the demon and thrown upon the earth, a prey to the most frightful convulsions. The venerable abbot hastened to put himself in prayer, begging relief for the unfortunate religious. Soon the demon, tormented in his turn, began to cry out: 'What have I done? What have I done? I was on the lettuce; she did not banish me from it, and she ate it.' In the name of Jesus Christ, the holy abbot commanded him to go out of the body of that servant of God, and never dare to molest her again. The demon obeyed, and the religious was entirely cured."

Thus, then, facts speak as well as testimonies; pagan theology as well as Christian theology; the East like the West; antiquity like modern times; Porphyrius like St. Gregory. What authority can your companions oppose to this?

To say that mankind are *blockheads*, and the universal custom of blessing the food *an obsolete superstition*, is easy, polite, and above all, convincing. However, as I am never satisfied with words, tell them that if they can allege one reason worth a Monaco penny, to authorize them in not making use of the blessing at table, I promise to give each of them a bust in the Pantheon. In the meantime, it remains established that prayer before eating is a law of humanity; and that it has been reserved to our epoch to produce minds so strong as to find it glorious to liken themselves publicly, twice a day, to the dog, the cat and the crocodile.

I leave you with this truth, promising for to-morrow another point of view.

Mgr. J.J. Gaume

Twentieth Letter

The Sign of the Cross is a guide that conducts us—Necessity of a guide—State of man here below—The Sign of the Cross conducts man to his end by remembrance, and by imitation—Remembrance which it recalls—General remembrance—Particular remembrance Particular imitation

December 16th

My Dear Frederic,

Ennobled, instructed, enriched, protected by the Sign of the Cross, what remains for man to attain happily the end of his pilgrimage? It remains for him to find a sure guide to conduct him. Like the archangel Raphael, sent to accompany the young Tobias in his distant voyage, the Sign of the Cross presents itself, and offers to render to all, to you as well as me, dear friend, the same service. Such is the last point of view under which we shall consider this adorable sign.

TRAVELERS TOWARDS HEAVEN, THE SIGN OF THE CROSS IS A GUIDE THAT CONDUCTS US.

It is midnight; the thunder rolls on all sides, the rain falls in torrents, ferocious beasts issuing from their dens, roar and run in every direction. Objects can be distinguished only by the glare of the lightning. You are alone in the midst of your Black Forest, such as it was in the time of Cæsar, immense, horrible, without road, path, or habitation, a vast haunt of those great bears of Germany, the sight of which affrighted the Romans, even on the inaccessible steps of the Coliseum. What shall become of you? Do you not feel the necessity of a charitable guide, who, appearing suddenly beside you, shall reassure you by his presence, and take you by the hand to conduct you safe and sound into the midst of your family?

Feeble image of the reality! The Black Forest is the world;

the tempest, with its darkness, its thunders, dangers and terrors, is life. Where am I? Whither am I going? What road shall I take? Such are the questions addressed to himself by the terrified man in the midst of this night so full of anguish. The answer is not long delayed; it is whole and entire in the Sign of the Cross.

Again, the Church, full of solicitude, teaches him to make it even from his cradle. Explained by the voice of his mother, this eloquent sign dissipates all darkness, illuminates the way, and directs through life.

"Having come from God," it says to man, "you are returning to God. Image of God, who is love, you must return to Him by love. Love includes remembrance and imitation. To think of God, to imitate God; this is for you the way, the truth, and the life. Understand me, and you shall without difficulty, fulfill the two fundamental laws of your existence."

Nothing is more true than this language of the divine guide; some details will suffice to demonstrate this.

Remembrance

They say in France, as in Germany, as everywhere, to-day as four thousand years ago, that remembrance is the pulse of friendship. As long as the pulse beats, life exists. It is extinct when the pulse ceases to beat. In like manner, as long as the remembrance of the beloved object subsists, affection continues. It languishes when remembrance grows faint; it dies when it disappears. All this, as you know, is elementary. We are so fully convinced that remembrance is a sign, a cause, a condition of human affection, that friends never fail when parting to say: "Do not forget me; I will never forget you;" and to give tokens which, notwithstanding their absence, may preserve their mutual remembrance.

It is with the love of God as with human friendships. Remembrance is its sign, its soul, its life. The remembrance of God being the first law of our being, it behooved Infinite Wisdom to give us a means of accomplishing it. The law being universal, this means should be universal. The law being for all, rich and poor, learned and ignorant, men of leisure and men of labor, the means should be accessible to all. The law being fundamental, the means should be very powerful.

I have told you, dear Frederic, that the law of remembrance is a fundamental law of humanity. The justification of these words will show you, in a new light, the importance of the Sign of the Cross.

What the sun is in the physical world, God is in every respect, and still more, in the moral world. Suppose that instead of continuing to shed on the world his torrents of light and heat, the sun is suddenly extinguished; imagine what becomes of nature? At the same instant, vegetation is stopped, the rivers and seas become plains of ice, and the earth as hard as a rock. All the malicious animals, which light enchains in the depth of the forests, issue from their caverns, and, by terrific howlings, call one another to the slaughter. Trouble and terror seize upon man. Everywhere reign confusion, despair, death; a few days suffice to bring the world back to chaos. Let God, the necessary sun of intelligences, disappear; moral life immediately becomes extinct. All ideas of good and evil are effaced. Truth and error, justice and injustice, are confounded in the right of the strongest. In the midst of such thick darkness, all the hideous cupidities, all the sanguinary instincts slumbering in the heart of man, are aroused, let loose, and without fear as without remorse, contend for the mutilated fragments of fortunes, cities, and empires. War is everywhere;

the war of all against all, which makes the world a vast den of thieves and assassins.

This spectacle the eye of man has never seen, any more than he has seen the universe without the planet which vivifies it. But what he has seen is a world on which, like the sun veiled with thick clouds, the idea of God casts only an uncertain glimmer. Thence have proceeded endless gropings, foolish and immoral systems, gross and cruel superstitions, passions instead of laws, crimes instead of virtues, materialism at the base, despotism at the summit, egotism everywhere, with the combats of the gladiators, and the banquets of human flesh.

Less complete than among the pagans, the forgetfulness of God, produced, however, among the Jews, analogous effects. Twenty times, by the medium of His prophets, did the Lord attribute to this crime the iniquities of Jerusalem, and the chastisements with which she was overwhelmed. Now, Jerusalem, as you know, is the type of nations.

"Therefore thus saith the Lord: Who hath heard such horrible things as the virgin of Israel hath done to excess? . . . because she hath forgotten me . . . Thou hast walked in the way of thy sister Samaria, and I will give her cup into thy hand. Thou shalt drink thy sister's cup, deep and wide, and thou shalt become the scorn of nations."

"Thou shalt be drunk with sorrows, drunk with the cup of grief and sadness, with the cup of thy sister Samaria."

"And thou shalt drink it, and shalt drain it even to the dregs; and thou shalt devour the fragments thereof, and thou shalt rend thy breasts. . . . Because thou hast forgotten me, and hast cast me off behind thy back; thou shalt bear thy crime and the chastisement of thy crime." [Jerem. 18:13, 15. Ezech. 23:31, 35. Is. 57:11, etc, etc.]

Could any one characterize with greater energy the fatal consequences of forgetfulness of God? Now the enormity of a crime is measured by the sanctity of the law which it violates.

The remembrance of God is, then, the vital law of humanity. On this basis, calculate the importance of the Sign of the Cross, especially destined to keep alive in man this salutary remembrance.

I have said *especially*, and with reason. The Sign of the Cross is a vase filled with divine souvenirs. In making it, all those souvenirs are shed even into the very depths of my being. I necessarily remember the Father, I necessarily remember the Son, I necessarily remember the Holy Ghost. I remember the Father as Creator, the Son as Redeemer, the Holy Ghost as sanctifier.

The Father recalls to you, as to me, as to every one who has a mind to understand, and a heart to love, all the divine benefits in the order of creation. I exist, and it is to Thee, O Father of fathers, that I owe life; life the basis of all natural gifts, that life which Thou hast given to me in preference to so many millions of possible beings. I owe to Thee the conservation of life. Each beating of my heart is a benefit. Thou renewest it every instant of the day and the night. Thou dost continue it during long years, notwithstanding my ingratitude, notwithstanding the bad use that I make of it. Thou dost continue it to me in preference to so many who, born with me, after me, are dead before me. I owe to Thee all that preserves, consoles, and beautifies life; and the sun that enlightens me, the air that I breathe, the earth that sustains me, the animals that serve me, the garments that cover me, the remedies that heal me, my parents, my friends, my body with its senses, my soul with its faculties, and all creatures visible and invisible, placed so magnificently at my service. O Father Creator, I owe all to Thee. The Son recalls all the divine benefits in the order of Redemption. When I pronounce Thy name, O adorable Son, it transports me into the splendors of eternity. There I behold Thee equal to the Father, seated upon the same throne, happy with an infinite felicity. Then, suddenly, I descend into a poor stable, before a wretched crib, and there I behold Thee, a little infant, deprived of every thing, trembling with cold, lying on a little straw, scarcely warmed by the caresses of Thy Mother, and the breath of two beasts. From the crib, I come to the cross. What a spectacle! Thou, O my God, the Monarch of worlds, the King of angels and of men, art hanging on a gibbet, between heaven and earth, in the company of two thieves; Thy body torn, Thy members pierced, Thy head crowned with thorns, Thy face defiled with blood and spittle, and all this for love of me!

The cross conducts me to the tabernacle. Before my God annihilated, before my God become my bread; before my God become my prisoner, my servant, obedient to my voice, to the voice of a child; before this abridgement of all the miracles of love, my tongue remains mute. The tongues of men and angels are powerless to stammer anything of a mystery which only infinite love could have conceived.

The Holy Ghost recalls all the divine benefits in the order of sanctification. Consubstantial Love of the Father and the Son, it is to Thee that the world owes every thing. It owes to Thee the Incarnate Word, its Redeemer: *Qui conceptus est de Spiritu Sancto* (Who was conceived by the Holy Ghost). [Creed] It owes to Thee Mary His Mother: *Spiritus Sanctus superveniet in te* (The Holy Ghost shall come upon thee). [St. Luke 1:35] It owes to Thee the Holy Catholic Church, that other mother, who is for the world and for me what Mary is for Jesus: *Credo in Spiritum Sanctum, sanctam Ecclesiam* (I believe in the Holy Ghost, the Holy Church). [Creed] Her bowels have borne me, her milk has nourished me, her sacraments strengthen and heal me. To her I owe the Communion of Saints, that glorious society which places me, a vile creature, in intimate communication with the angelic hierarchies, with all the saints, from Abel down to the last of the elect. To her I owe the preservation of the Gospel, that luminous torch which has drawn the human race out of barbarism, and prevents it from returning to it again.

Do you know any souvenir so fruitful, so eloquent as the Sign of the Cross? The philosopher, the politician, the Christian, sometimes ask for books to meditate; here is one which can take the place of all others. This book, intelligible to all, legible to all, gratuitously given, is within the reach of every one. Such has God made it, and what He has made, He has made well.

Imitation

To remember God, is the first law of our being. You see, dear friend, the importance of this law, and how the Sign of the Cross helps us to accomplish it. To imitate God, is another law no less fundamental. On this point, a reasonable mind never entertains the least doubt. Is not every being obliged to tend to its perfection? Is it not for this, and for this alone, that life has been given to it? What then can be the perfection of a being, if it does not consist in its resemblance to the type on which it has been formed? Is not the picture so much the more perfect, as it better expresses the traits of the model? Man is made to the image of God. To copy trait for trait this divine Prototype, to assign to his perfection no other bounds than the perfection of his sublime Model; such is the law of his being, and the obligatory labor of his entire life.

"I have given you the example," said the God-Man, "that as I myself have done, so you do also." And His great apostle: "Be you imitators of me, as I myself am of the Incarnate Word; no salvation for those who shall not be found conformed to the divine type."

Now nothing is more fit to guide us in this way of imitation than the Sign of the Cross. What does man do in forming it? He pronounces the name of God, for God is the Father, the Son, and the Holy Ghost, three distinct Persons in one and the same Divinity. By repeating to man the name of God, the Sign of the Cross places before his eyes his Eternal Model, the Being by excellence, in whom are united all perfections in an infinite degree.

Again, in repeating the name of each person of the august Trinity, it proposes to our imitation the particular perfections of each. In the Father, infinite power, and it says to me: You must imitate the power of the Father, Creator and Moderator of all things, by the government of yourself and the world; by the empire over your passions, over the maxims, customs, interests, fashions, threats and promises, contrary to the liberty and dignity of a child of God, a king like his Father.

In the Son, infinite wisdom, and it says to me: You must imitate the wisdom of the Son, by the justness of your appreciations and judgments; by the preference invariably given to the soul over the body, to eternity over time, duty over pleasure, to riches that remain over goods that pass away.

In the Holy Ghost, infinite love, and it says to me: You must imitate the charity of the Holy Ghost, by regulating and ennobling your affections, by tearing from your heart even the last fibre of egotism, jealousy, hatred, and all the vices which produce degradation within, and trouble without.

What do you think of it? Is not the Sign of the Cross an excellent guide? Where is the professor of philosophy who can flatter himself with showing more clearly the way of perfection? Nevertheless, we have learned only one part of its teachings; the others to-morrow.

Mgr. J.J. Gaume

Twenty-first Letter

General imitation — Imitation of the sanctity of God — What sanctity is — The Sign of the Cross, the sanctifier of man and of creatures — Imitation of the charity of God — What charity is in God — What it should be in us — In teaching it to us, the Sign of the Cross is an eloquent and sure guide — Incontestable proofs

December 18th

Dear Friend,

Thanks to the Sign of the Cross, each person of the adorable Trinity places Himself, in some sort, before us, that we may copy Him. Under the great name of God, They offer to our imitation all perfections united. From among them I choose two, shining more brilliantly, and more necessary to be imitated now than ever: sanctity and charity.

Sanctity. — Sanctity means unity, freedom from all foreign mixture. God is holy, because He is one. He is thrice holy, because He is thrice one. One in power, because it is infinite; one in wisdom, because it is infinite; one in love, because it is infinite. In God nothing limits, nothing alters this triple unity. He is holy, perfectly holy, completely holy in Himself, for the reason I have just alleged.

He is holy in His works. In none can He suffer guilty mixture, disorder, or to call it by its true name, sin. The angels falling from heaven, man expelled from the terrestrial paradise, the world drowned by the deluge, Sodom consumed by fire, the Roman empire falling under the blows of barbarians, the great Victim of Calvary crucified between two thieves, calamities public or private, hell with its eternal fires; all are so many testimonies of the inexorable sanctity of God in His creatures. It is a great lesson, which the Sign of the Cross incessantly gives us. I cannot make it, but it says to me: Image of a God holy, thrice holy, inexorably holy, you yourself must be holy, thrice holy, inexorably holy, in your memory, your understanding, your will.

Holy in my soul and body, holy in myself and my works, whether alone or in company, young or old, powerful or feeble, holy in all, holy everywhere, holy always; such is the divine unity which I must realize in myself. "O, man!" exclaims Tertullian, "how great thou art, if thou dost comprehend thyself!" *O homo, tantum nomen si intelligas te!*

This is not enough; like God Himself, I must realize it outwardly. Over all that surrounds me should be spread the sanctity or unity of my life. Examples, words, prayers, nothing in me which does not serve to remove the evil, the dualism from my neighbor, like me, the image of God, like me, created for unity.

In this obligation, so vividly recalled by the Sign of the Cross, do those prodigies of devotedness, incessantly renewed in the bosom of Catholicity, take their origin.

Ask our legions of apostles of both sexes, what it is that leads them to place at the service of unknown barbarians, intellects the most noble, lives the most pure, blood the most generous. All will reply: The words of the Master. We have heard the Word, the Redeemer, ordaining that all the members of the human family should be marked with the august Sign of the Trinity. Immortal as Himself, this word resounds in our hearts, and wherever there is a forehead still unmarked by the liberating sign, we hasten, we work, we die.

Hear the general-in-chief of those heroic legions, Xavier, the St. Paul of modern times. You know that, by his gigantic labors, this wonderful man conquered a world to civilization and the faith. But what powerful lever raised his courage and that of his successors, even to temerity; his ambition and theirs, even to enthusiasm and folly? *O sanctissima Trinitas!* (O Most Holy Trinity!) This war-cry, almost as frequent as respiration on the lips of Xavier, reveals to you the common thought. With an eye illumined by faith, the apostle considers the numerous nations of India, China, and Japan. He sees them seated in the shadow of death, and bearing on their dishonored brows the sign of the beast, instead of the glorious character of the Trinity. At this spectacle of utter degradation his zeal is inflamed, and from his heaving breast escapes the war-cry, *O sanctissima Trinitas!* O Most Holy Trinity!

What dishonor for Thee! What misfortune for the work of Thy hands! And to repair those disfigured images by engraving on their foreheads the divine sign, Xavier rushes forward like a giant. Space diminishes beneath his feet. He laughs at dangers, and places no other bounds to his repairing ambition than the limits of the world. Even the world itself seems too little for his heart, and his travels are equal to three times its circumference. [Life of St. Fr. Xavier, t. ii., lib. vi. pp. 208-213.]

Although death does not permit him to go through it in every sense, yet he points out to his successors the nations to be conquered. His desire is accomplished. Borne on the wings of the wind, according to Fenelon's expression, thousands of missionaries shall arrive in every isle, every forest, every region, however distant, however inhospitable it may be.

Their first care shall be to reestablish, on the forehead of man, sunk even into cannibalism, the sanctifying Sign of the Cross, repeating, like their chief: *O sanctissima Trinitas!* That such is the motive which animates evangelical conquerors, is proved by the fact that all their ministry consists in marking the infidel nations with the seal of the adorable Persons, and afterwards in maintaining inviolate the divine resemblance.

The Sign of the Cross does yet more. It sanctifies all that it touches, man or creatures. Now, in sanctifying creatures after having sanctified man, the divine guide leads all things back to their end, unity. It is an article of universal faith that religious signs have power to modify inanimate creatures: we have seen it in all that precedes. Because it is universal, such a belief cannot be false. The great Mistress of truth regards it as part of the deposit confided to her care. Each day she practices it, and teaches the practice of it.

See the Catholic Church during eighteen centuries and in every part of the globe, sanctifying by the Sign of the Cross, water, salt, oil, bread, wax, stone, wood, and all insensible creatures.

What is it, theologically, to say that the Sign of the Cross sanctifies man and creatures? In regard of man, I do not pretend that the Sign of the Cross confers on him sanctifying grace, or that it is an instrument proper to confer it, like the sacraments. I mean that it communicates a kind of sanctification, like that of the catechumen on whom this divine sign is made before baptism: "For," says St. Augustine, "there are sanctifications of many kinds." [Lib. ii. De Peccat. merit. et remiss., c. cxxvi.]

The Sign of the Cross is an act to which God attaches the application of the merits of His son, without, however, giving it the virtue of baptism or penance. Almsgiving is not a sacrament; and nevertheless, it is something good, pious, salutary and sanctifying.

As to creatures, to sanctify an inanimate thing, is it not to give it a physical and inherent quality? Is it not to bring it back to its native purity, and communicate to it a virtue superior to its nature? From this proceed two effects of sanctification.

The first purifies creatures in this sense, that it frees them from the influences of the demon. The second renders them proper to produce effects beyond their natural strength. Thus modified, they become, in the hands of man, instruments of healing, arms against the demons, preservatives against dangers of soul and body.

How many miraculous events, public and private, ancient and modern, could we cite as due to those creatures; irrational, indeed, but sanctified by the Sign of the Cross. If, instead of wasting their time in dabbling in pagan fables, and legends of Rome and Greece, the rising generations would study the history of the Church and the lives of the saints, your companions would know, on this point, many facts better proved than those of Alexander and Socrates. [See Gretzer, p. 696, et suiv.]

It is not by the imitation of the divine sanctity alone, but of the divine charity also, that the Sign of the Cross, as an eloquent and sure guide, places us, keeps and sustains us in our way.

Charity.—God, Whose children we are, and Whose images we ought to be, is charity; *Deus caritas est*. [1 Jn IV, 8] This word tells everything. It tells what God is in Himself and in His works. The Father being God, is charity. The Son being God, is charity. The Holy Ghost being God, is charity. The Trinity whole and entire, is charity. God is charity! Do you know a name more beautiful? And the Sign of the Cross, each time that we make it, repeats this to our hearts.

Charity means union and effusion. Between the three august Persons all is union and unity: unity of power, unity of thoughts, unity of operations, unity of happiness, unity of essence. Even the shadow of a discord never troubles this perfect, this ravishing harmony. Why? Because one only love, a love, full, eternal and unalterable, is the delightful bond of the Trinity.

Effusion.—Essentially communicative, charity tends to spread itself abroad, and infinite charity, with infinite strength and abundance. Now, the exterior works of God are creation, conservation, redemption, sanctification, and glorification.

Now to create is to love; to conserve is to love; to redeem is to love; to sanctify is to love; to glorify is to love. All charity comes from the heart. God is, then, a heart. Do you know a name more delightful? And this name the Sign of the Cross repeats to us every time we make it.

God is charity. To you as to me, as to every man, whatever be his age or condition, this word tells what we ought to be. Images of God, we should resemble Him. To resemble Him is to be charity, charity in ourselves and in our works. In ourselves, by the supernatural bond of grace which unites among themselves all our faculties, ennobles them, strengthens one by the other, and causes all to tend to the same end, the formation of the perfect resemblance between God and us.

In our works, by the Divine principle, which, uniting us to all men, as members of the same body, makes our heart beat in unison with theirs, and sheds its salutary effusions on all that belongs to them, thus realizing the last wish of Our Divine Master: "O Father! that they may be one as we also are one."

I stop, my dear Frederic, at these points, which you can easily develop. They suffice to show the importance of the Sign of the Cross as the guide of man. If your comrades have the misfortune to doubt it, propose to them the following questions:

Is it true or not, that nothing is more calculated to remind us of God and the Trinity than the Sign of the Cross?

Is it true or not, that man is formed to the image of God?

Is it true or not, that the first duty, and the natural tendency of any being whatever, is to reproduce in itself the type after which it has been made?

Is it true or not, that if man does not make persevering efforts to form himself to the image of God, he inevitably forms himself to the image of the demon, and of his unruly passions; so that in not becoming, day by day, more holy, more charitable, more like God, he daily becomes more perverse, more egotistical, more like the demon, more of a beast, *animalis homo* (beastly man)?

Is it true or not, that man continually tends, either with or without his knowledge, to make all that surrounds him like himself, and that from each permanent action proceeds sanctification or perversion, order or disorder, the salvation or the ruin of individuals, families, societies, beliefs and morals?

However little they may have of logic, and above all, of impartiality, their answer, I have no doubt, will be what it should. With us they must conclude that nothing is better founded, or, to use the language of the day, more profoundly philosophical, than the frequent, and very frequent use of the Sign of the Cross. They will conclude that neither the primitive Christians, nor the true Christians of every age, nor the Catholic Church, nor in fine, the élite of humanity have been deceived in invariably preserving the use of this mysterious sign. They will conclude that error, blame and disgrace belong to the despisers of the Sign of the Cross; that in not making it, in being ashamed to make it, in laughing at those who make it, they rank themselves with the refuse of humanity, degrade

themselves beneath the pagans, and liken themselves to beasts.
What remains, then, for them and for us?
In my last letters, you shall learn it.

Mgr. J.J. Gaume

Twenty-second Letter

Sentence of the judgment between us and the first Christians — First obligation, to make the Sign of the Cross boldly, to make it often, and to make it well — Reasons for making it boldly — Disgrace and danger of not making it — State of the physical and moral health of the world at the present day

December 19th

Dear Frederic,

When, in civil affairs, a judgment without appeal is rendered, what remains to the parties? Only one thing. Under pain of revolt and all the consequences of revolt, it must be executed. It is the same in doctrinal questions. When an infallible authority has pronounced upon a point in litigation, only one course remains. Under pain of a revolt much more grievous, and all the consequences of that revolt, the decree of the supreme tribunal must be taken as the rule of conduct.

A trial was instituted between us and the early Christians. It was to be decided who were right and or wrong; the first Christians who made the Sign of the Cross, made it very often, and made it well; or modern Christians who do not make the Sign of the Cross, make it seldom, or make it badly. The cause has been carefully examined, the debates published, the pleadings heard. The élite of humanity, constituted as a sovereign tribunal, and having for assistant judges, faith, reason, experience, and nations, even those which were pagan, have decided in favor of the Christians of the primitive Church. What remains for us to do? We must renew the glorious chain of our ancient traditions, so unhappily broken, and make the Sign of the Cross boldly, make it often, make it well.

Make the Sign of the Cross boldly and openly. And why should we not do so? Why be ashamed of making it? Remark well, my dear friend, that to make, or not make the Sign of the Cross, is not an optional thing. He who makes it honors himself; he who does not make it, dishonors himself.

In making the Sign of the Cross, we have behind us, around us, with us, all the great men and grand ages of the East and West; all the immortal Catholic nation, the élite of humanity. In not making it, we have behind us, around us, with us, the shallow-minded heretics, unbelievers, and ignoramuses, the little and great beasts. In making the Sign of the Cross we cover both ourselves and creatures with an invincible armor. In not making it, we disarm ourselves, and expose both ourselves and creatures to the gravest perils.

Both man and the world necessarily live under the influence of the Spirit of good or the spirit of evil. Master of man and of creatures, the spirit of evil makes them feel his malignant influence; body and soul, mind and matter are vitiated by it. This fundamental truth has been believed by all mankind.

Again, for more than eighteen centuries the chiefs of the eternal combat have not ceased to cry out to us with one voice, to cover both ourselves and creatures with the Sign of the Cross, a buckler, impenetrable to the burning darts of the enemy: *Scutum in quo ignitæ diaboli extinguuntur sagittæ.* And we, soldiers unfaithful to our instructions, voluntarily cast aside our armor? With naked breast, we stupidly remain exposed to the deadly blows of the armed enemy! And all this, that we may not displease *others*; and such *others*! But they say: "The present world does not make the Sign of the Cross, and it is none the worse for it." Is this quite certain? What is to-day the general health of man and of nature? Do you not hear it repeated every day in Germany as in France, as everywhere, "There is no more health?" This saying, now become popular, is it no more than a saying? Even optimists tell it to you. Do you believe then that the divine laws made for man, mind and matter, have not in this life a double sanction, one moral, the other physical? Do you believe that the profanation, becoming more and more general, of the days consecrated to the repose of man and creatures, the contempt of the laws of fast and abstinence, the abandonment of the Bread of Life, can compromise only the salvation of the soul?

Do you believe that the over-anxiety of affairs, the agitations of politics, the fever of enjoyments, distinctive character of a world which has undertaken to make heaven descend upon earth; the effeminacy of manners, the abnormal habit of turning night into day and day into night, the searches of sensuality in food, the frightful consumption of alcoholic liquors, our five hundred thousand coffeehouses and taverns, are without influence on the public health? Whence, then proceeds the diminution of strength in modern generations? Would it be easy to find, to-day, many young men capable of handling the arms of our ancestors of the middle ages, or even of carrying their armor?

Those numerous reforms, made by the councils of revision on account of etiolation (weakening or enfeeblement) or defects of conformation; the inability of so many persons, even religious, to observe the law of fasting, although so much mitigated, have they no signification? What says that augmentation, already considerable yet ever increasing, of apothecaries, physicians, health officers and *healing mediums*, whose antechambers will soon be as much frequented as the offices of the most eminent medical men?

Finally, those cases of suicide and insanity, which in our time have swelled to such unprecedented numbers, and are still increasing, are they very reassuring symptoms of the public health? Even allowing to them only a limited value, do these facts and many others, demonstrate that the man of to-day is no worse than the man of former times? And the health of nature, over which is no longer made the liberating sign, is it still improving? What means the disease of the potatoes, the disease of the vine, the diseases of trees, vegetables, plants, and herbs, even of pasture? All these unhealthy plants, which number more than one hundred, attacked simultaneously by serious, unknown and obstinate diseases, do they prove the perfect health of creatures? This phenomenon, all the more inauspicious, as it is *without analogy in history*, does it not rather seem to give to actual nature the appearance of a great hospital, in which, like the human species, all suffers, all languishes, all dies?[*]

---

[*] I will here give you a list of the trees, shrubs, plants, and vegetables, actually diseased, indicating at the same time the maladies which destroy them. S, indicates *lepis*, or spots. O, *oidium*. R, rust or blast. I, *insects*: small worms lodged on or beneath the surface of the leaves.

TREES.

Oak, S. I.	Chestnut, S.	Pear, S. I.
Beech, S.I.	Maple, S.	Cherry, S.
Elm, S. R. I.	Willow, S. R.	Plum, S.
Birch, S. I.	Ebony, S. I.	Apricot, S. O.
Ash, S. I.	Linden, S.	Mulberry, S. O.
Poplar, (Italian) S. I.	Plane, S.	Orange, S. O.
Poplar, (Canadian) S. R.	Apple, S. I.	Vine, S. O.

SHRUBS.

Rose, S. R. O. I.	Gooseberry, S. I.	Snowball, S.
Hawthorn, S. O. I.	Ribes nigrum et rubrum, S.	Wezelia, S.
Glicynia cinensis, S.	Berberis vulgaris, O.	Syringa vulgaris, S.
Raspberry, S. R.	Lilac, S. I.	Althæa, S. I.
Blackberry, S. R. O.	Jasmine, S.	Filbert, S. I.

It cannot then be denied; considered in man, and in creatures immediately subjected to man, the world of our day

---

Eglantine, O.	Elder, S.		Osier, S. R.

PLANTS.

Peonies of different species, S.		Phlox, S.	Dandelion, S.
Millefolium, S. O.		Daisy, S.	Gladiola, S. R.
Campanula, R.		Erythrina, S.	Chicory, S. R. O.
Thistle, S. O.		Queen of the meadow, S.	Scabious, S.
Wild plants of dif. species, S. R. O.		Diclytra spectabilis, S.	Long Dragon, R.
Chamomile, S.	Violet, S.	Primrose, S	Heliotrope, S.

VEGETABLES.

Wheat, S. R.	Potatoes, S.	Sorrel, R.	Bean, S. R.
Rye, R.	Kidney Beans, S. R.	Cabbage, S. R.	Clover, S.O.
Oats, S. R.	Salsify, R.	Turnip, R. I.	Bulrush, S. R.
Barley, R.	Celery, R.	Beet root, R.	Reed, R.
Field herbs of different kinds, R.		Wild herbs of dif. kinds, S. R. O.	

We owe the above list to the kindness of M. F. Verecruysse de Courtrai. He himself collected, in 1862, leaves of all the diseased plants, of which he has been kind enough to send us specimens. We beg him to allow us to offer him the public expression of our gratitude. Material creatures being incapable of either good or evil, are diseased only by resilience; they follow the condition of man. Man being the centre and abridgment of the creation, encloses within himself all the laws which regulate inferior creatures. If he violates them, the consequences of his violation are felt by all nature. Witness the sin of Adam. To the like cause, reproduced in the course of ages, we must attribute the maladies of creatures, always in direct proportion to the cause which produces them. Does it not seem as if Isaiah was looking forward to our epoch when he wrote: "The earth is infected by the inhabitants thereof. From thence tears, mourning, weakness of the earth, decay of the world; the malady of the vine, and the mourning of the cultivators." Luxit et defluxit terra, et infirmata est . . . de fluxit orbis . . . et terra infecta ut ab habitatoribus suis, quia . . . Mutaverunt Jus . . . propter hoc . . . infirmata est vitis etc. (XXIV, 4, ana foll.) Habacuc, Jeremias and the other prophets speak in the same terms of this agony of nature.

is diseased, more diseased than formerly. But what is the malady? It is the enfeebling of life. The Word Creator is life and all life. To approach Him is to augment life, to retire from Him is to diminish it. In the judgment of the Church and all Christian ages, the exterior act, the feature of union the most universal and most ordinary which places man and creatures in contact with the Life, is the Sign of the Cross. Now, you laugh at it, you do not make it; you do not wish to make it. As far as you are concerned, you replace it, and also the prayers and pilgrimages of former times, by sea-bathing, by waters hot, cold, tepid, or sulphureous, from Vichy, Switzerland, Germany, or the Pyrenees. And in creatures, by artificial manure, *echenillage*, (ridding of caterpillars), draining, and sulphur. All very well; only it is necessary to do the one, and not omit the other: *Hæc oportuit facere et illa non omittere* (These things you ought to have done and not to leave those undone). [St. Matthew XXIII, 23]

Thus the people of the world of our day, despisers of wisdom both human and divine, believe that they can violate with impunity a law religiously observed from the foundation of Christianity, and respected even by the pagans, who had it as a formula in the celebrated maxim: *Orandum est ut sit mens sana in corpore sano*, (It is necessary to pray in order to enjoy physical and moral health). Let us not complain; we have what we have, and it is our due. Even were the physical health of man and nature, bereft of the Sign of the Cross, to be as flourishing as they pretend, there would still remain the moral health, far more important than the first. Now, what is the sanitary state of souls in the world of our day? The answer would lead me too far. I only remind you that the moral man, as well as the physical, has the inevitable alternative either to live under the salutary influence of the good Spirit, or the malevolent influence of the evil spirit. The Sign of the Cross places us under the first; the absence of this sign abandons us to the second. Such is, again, the teaching of the Church, confirmed by the practice of Christian ages.

This experience of eighteen hundred years is nothing to you. You no longer want the sacred sign; you no longer have any faith in it; you no longer make it on your forehead, your lips, your heart, your food. Ah, well! the demon will mark his own. On all those foreheads, on all those lips, on all those hearts, on all that food, shall be seen, without any necessity for a microscope, the sign of the beast.

What is the sign of the beast on the forehead? It is pride, insubordination, anger, contempt, effrontery, agitation of the features; inaptitude for spiritual sciences, disgust for moral studies; pleasures tarnished by the vice of impurity or consumed by wine; something heavy in the countenance; something low, dull and bestial; the cynicism of eyes full of adultery, full of a sin that never ends, continually alluring unstable souls. [I Cor. 11,14; 2 Pet. 11,14.]

What is it on the lips? Laughter, either immodest or immoderate, foolishly impious or cruelly mocking; talkativeness without rule, without importance, without aim, obscene words, words of deceit, irreligion, blasphemy, hatred detraction and jealousy; too full of concupiscences which rise like a foam, infectious as the exhalations of a sepulchre, deadly as the venom of a viper. [Ps. 5, 11. Jud. 13.]

What is it in the heart? Bad thoughts, wicked desires, fornications, impurities, treasons, the shameful littlenesses of egotism; thefts, poisonings, murders, [St. Matth. xv. 19, etc.] the reign of courtesans, the apotheosis of actresses.

What is it over eatables? Their pernicious influence. Not having been delivered by the saving sign, they serve, as even the pagans themselves acknowledged, as vehicles to the demon. Placed by manducation (eating) in intimate contact with the inferior part of the soul, they excite its appetites, flatter its base instincts, and stir up its passions.

Hence, what we now see; nicety in choice, sensuality in eating and drinking, despotism of the flesh, disgust for labor, powerlessness to resist temptation, the abasement and sometimes brutalizing of the intellect, softness of morals, Sybaritism (indulgent fondness of sensuous luxury) of habits, the adoration of the god of the belly, completed to-day more than ever by contempt of self, by the stifling of conscience and the moral sense, by suicide and infanticide. [Philip. iii. 18.] Look around you, my dear friend; seek for countenances, lips, hearts and tables, where are preserved the health, dignity, and sobriety of the man and the Christian; lives pure and mortified; lives strong against temptations, lives devoted to virtue and charity, lives which may, without shame, be revealed to friends or enemies; you will find them only under the protection of the Sign of the Cross.

What I have told you to-day, accept as a fact of experience. To-morrow I will give you the reasons and proofs of it.

Mgr. J.J. Gaume

Twenty-third Letter

Reasons of the power and exalted mission of the Sign of the Cross—Fundamental dogma—What happens in the political order a figure of what takes place in the moral order—The Reformation, first daughter of Paganism, throws down all crosses—The French Revolution, second daughter of Paganism, imitates her sister—Second obligation, to make the Sign of the Cross frequently—Reasons drawn from our present state—Third obligation, to make it well, condition—The Sign of the Cross, eternal sign of victory—Constantine—Praises of the Sign of the Cross

December 20th

My Dear Frederic,

You do not forget, my dear Frederic, that we draw practical conclusions from the judgment rendered between us and our ancestors. The first is, that we should make the Sign of the Cross courageously.

Although the decision of a tribunal without appeal suffices to determine our conduct, I have wished, in order to render it more worthy of respect, to show you the shame, the dangers and misfortunes which would be the consequence of a revolt, either theoretical or practical. Facts have spoken. You have seen the sign of the beast engraven on those foreheads, hearts, lips and aliments, unsanctified by the divine sign. Whence does this proceed? I have promised to tell you.

The sign of the beast is inevitably imprinted on man, and on every thing unprotected by the Sign of the Cross, the liberator of man and the world: it cannot be, it never shall be otherwise. As for the world there is but one lightning-conductor, so for man there is but one preservative against the demon,—it is the Sign of the Cross. Where *it* is not, there satan is master.

This fact, as we have repeatedly seen, holds to the most

profound, and, altogether, the most incontestable dogma of humanity; *the servitude of man and the world to the spirit of evil since the original fall.* To render more palpable what I say of the exalted mission of the Sign of the Cross, allow me to remind you of some historical facts, too seldom noticed.

What happens in the political world is but a reflection of what takes place in the moral. Now when a dynasty ascends the throne, its first care is to erect its standard and engrave its coat-of-arms everywhere. This is the sign of its sovereignty. Does it happen to be overthrown? The first act of the conqueror is to destroy the emblems of the vanquished dynasty, and replace them by his own. Thus is announced to the eyes of the people the inauguration of a new reign. How many times during the last seventy years have we seen in France and elsewhere, this change of colors and escutcheons! In coming to take possession of His kingdom, the Incarnate Word found satan the king and god of the world. The statues, trophies, coat-of-arms, and insignia of the usurper were everywhere. He being vanquished, all those signs of his sovereignty disappeared. In their place shone the arms of the Victor, the cross. When, for its crimes, a soul or a country is again abandoned to satan, and he takes possession of it, the first act of the usurper is to cause the Sign of the Cross to disappear. Then it is, and only then, that having no longer to fear this formidable sign, he acts therein as master.

Read again one page in the history of your own country. From 1520 to 1530, what spectacle does Germany present to you? From the Rhine to the Danube, all those crosses which, from the victory of Christianity over Scandinavian idolatry, had crowned the hills and mountains, bordered the roads, enameled the fields, ornamented the tops of houses, shone on the summits of churches, decorated the apartments of the rich, or consoled the cottages of the poor, were thrown down, broken into fragments, cast to the winds, or dragged in the mire, amidst the vociferations of a delirious people. What did that destructive storm announce? The advent of the victor, the re-establishment of his reign. Since that time the spirit of darkness has ruled Germany. There, as in the ancient world, he reigns by despotism, voluptuousness, cruelty, and robbery, by the confusion of right and wrong, by intellectual anarchy, under every name and form.

We find the like spectacle in Prussia, Saxony, Holland, Denmark, Sweden, Norway, England, Switzerland, and every country where the usurper has taken the place of the rightful King. This fact is the more significant, as it is not isolated in history. We see it reproduced every time that satan retakes possession of a country. It gives the character of the infernal victory, whether general or particular, slow or rapid, and measures its extent.

In 1830 the crosses thrown down might be counted only by hundreds; 1830 was an abortion of 1793. In the latter epoch, epoch of the complete triumph of paganism, it was far otherwise. By thousands might be counted the crosses thrown down and broken on the soil of France. In that time of sad, yet instructive remembrances, there is one day, inauspicious beyond all others. The tenth of August, 1792, saw the throne and altar sink in blood, under the blows of fanatical hordes. The massacres of the Carmes and St. Firmin, the proclaiming of the Republic, the assassination of Louis XVI., the hecatombs of the Reign of Terror, the filthiness of the Directory, the apostasies and sacrileges, the goddesses of Reason, were only the consequences of that lamentable day. It shall eternally mark the precise hour in which satan made his triumphant entry into the most Christian kingdom.

"Now, at that moment," writes an historian of the period, "a fearful storm, such as had never been seen, burst over Paris. All day a heavy, dead heat had stifled respiration. Gloomy clouds, marbled, towards evening, with sinister-looking streaks, had appeared to engulf the sun in a suspended ocean. Towards ten o'clock the electricity discharged itself by thousands of flashes of lightning, like luminous palpitations of the heavens. The winds, imprisoned behind that ridge of clouds, burst forth, roaring like the waves, bending the harvests, breaking the branches of the trees, and carrying away roofs of dwellings. The rain and hail rang on the ground as if the earth were being stoned from above. The houses were closed, the streets and roads deserted in an instant. The lightning, which, during eight successive hours, did not cease to flash and strike, killed a great number of those men and women who came during the night to provision Paris. Some of the sentinels were found struck amidst the ashes of their sentry boxes. Iron gates, twisted by the wind and the fire of heaven, were torn from the walls to which they had been fastened by hinges, and carried to an incredible distance. Montmarte and Mont Valerien, the two natural domes which rise above the horizon of the suburbs of Paris, discharged in greater surface the fluid accumulated in the clouds which enveloped them. The lightning, attacking by preference all those monuments standing alone or crowned with iron, *threw down all the crosses* erected in the country, on the roads and cross-roads, from the plain of Issy to the woods of St. Germain and Versailles, even to the cross of the bridge of Charenton. The next day the limbs of those crosses were everywhere scattered over the ground, *as if an invisible army had, in its passage, overthrown all the repudiated signs of Christian worship."*

There is no more chance in the moral order than there are leaps in nature. The facts I have just related, have then a signification. Now, the circumstances which have accompanied and followed them, prove evidently, the cause of the existence or non-existence of the Sign of the Cross in a country. They also prove to nations, provinces, cities, countries, and men, whoever they may be, how much it imports them to preserve, multiply, and honor that sign, the protector of the whole creation.

To make the Sign of the Cross frequently, is the second practical consequence of the judgment rendered. And why should we not make it? Why not, each one, as far as he is concerned, return to the practice of our forefathers? They did not believe themselves secure even for an instant, even in the most ordinary actions of life, if they were not protected by the salutary sign. Are we stronger than they? Are our temptations less numerous, less active? our dangers less pressing? our obligations less serious?

Every time that our fathers went out of their dwellings, their eyes were offended by the sight of statues, pictures, obscene objects, customs, and feasts, wherein the spirit of evil appeared on all sides. What discourses, what conversations, what songs fell on their chaste ears! Under every form the most seductive, the sensualism and naturalism of ideas and morals, both public and private, were a permanent conspiracy against the supernaturalism of their life, against their spirit of mortification, simplicity, poverty, and detachment. Moreover, they had to defend their faith against the sarcasms, the contempt, and the sophisms of nations and of pagan philosophy. They had to answer for it before judges, and attest it in amphitheatres.

In order to preserve themselves amidst so many perils, what was their secret? The Sign of the Cross, always the Sign of the Cross. And we Catholics of the nineteenth century, what is our condition? Has not every thing, or nearly every thing that surrounds us again become pagan? Where shall we find one word of the Gospel in the greater number of men and things? Are not the cities of modern Europe like those of former times, filled with statues, paintings, engravings, and objects capable of enkindling in the most frigid souls the impure fires of concupiscence?

In streets, in parlors, and in daily lectures, what strikes upon our ears? What does the modern world need, to be entirely pagan in the luxury of its table, furniture, lodging, garments and enjoyments? Slavery and wealth. The instincts are the same as in the days of the Cæsars! Is not such a spectacle a continual snare? Woe to him who does not see it! Woe, above all, to him who does not watch daily over his heart and senses!

If it be difficult to defend our morals, what a war must we sustain in order to preserve our faith! Do we not live in a time in which false ideas, lies and sophisms, as numerous as the atoms of the air, are current in society? Everywhere are the amphitheatres in which we must combat for the Church, for our belief, our traditions, our customs, for Christian supernaturalism. The arena is never closed; one combat is sooner ended than another begins.

Placed in a like condition with us, the early Christians were acquainted with a weapon, victorious, universal, and familiar to all, of which they made constant use; it was the Sign of the Cross. Have we a better? Ah, if ever it was necessary to make the protecting sign upon ourselves and our creatures, it is to-day. What prevents us from imitating our ancestors? How can it be incompatible with our occupations to make the Sign of the Cross on the heart, or, after the ancient manner, on the forehead with the thumb, or on the mouth with the thumb and the index? If we be vanquished, whose will be the fault? *Perditio tua ex te Israël* (Destruction is thy own, O Israel)! [Hosea 13:9]

To make the Sign of the Cross well, is the third application of the sentence pronounced. Regularity, respect, attention, confidence, and devotion should accompany our hand when it forms the adorable sign.

Regularity. It requires that the Sign of the Cross, in its perfect form, be made according to the traditional law, that is to say, with the right hand and not the left; by slowly carrying the hand from the forehead to the breast, from the breast to the left shoulder, and then to the right, while pronouncing the name of the three persons of the august Trinity. [Navarr., Comment. de Orat. et horis canon. c. xix, n. 200.]

Nothing of this is arbitrary. If they were to come forth from their tombs, it is thus the Christians of the apostolic times would make the Sign of the Cross. Let us hear an eye-witness.

"We make the Sign of the Cross with the right hand over the catechumens," says St. Justin, "because the right hand is accounted more noble than the left, although it differs from it only in position, and not in its nature; thus we pray turned toward the east, as being the most noble part of creation. From whom did the Church receive this manner of prayer? From those who taught her to pray; from the Apostles." [Quæst., xviii.]

We have a curious passage from St. Augustine on the dignity of the right hand. "Do you not reprove," says he, "him who eats with the left hand? If you look on the guest who eats with the left hand as offering an insult to your table, why should it not be an insult to the divine table, to make with the left hand what should be made with the right, and with the right what should be made with the left." [In Psal. 136.] St. Gregory adds: "Such is the manner of speaking among men; we call noble and precious what is at the right, less precious, less noble what is at the left. [Moral., lib. xx. c. 18.]

As to the words which accompany the movement of the hand, they, also, are of apostolic tradition. "Over all that you meet," says St. Ephrem, "make the Sign of the Cross, in the Name of the Father, and of the Son, and of the Holy Ghost." [De Baptism, c. vi.]

And Tertullian: "Faith is signed in the Father, and in the Son, and in the Holy Ghost." [De panoplia.]

And St. Alexander, soldier and martyr under Maximian, on being condemned to death, turned toward the east, made the Sign of the Cross three times over his body and said: "Glory be to Thee, O God of our fathers, Father and Son and Holy Ghost." [Apud Sur, May 13.]

However, the form which I have just described was less in use among the primitive Christians than it is among us. Their ordinary way was to make the Sign of the Cross with the thumb on the forehead: *Frontem crucis signaculo terimus.* This was because of their fear of betraying themselves, and also on account of the incessant repetition of the adorable sign. Such is still the form most frequently employed in Spain and many other countries.[*]

---

[*] There are two ways of holding the hand in making the Sign of the Cross. The first consists in extending the first three fingers, and closing the other two. This manner, which distinctly expresses the mystery of the Holy

But why on the forehead rather than on the heart? Herein, my dear Frederic, as in all that is ancient, there are great mysteries. I count five.

The first, the honor of the Divine Crucified. "It is not without reason," says St. Augustine, "that the Incarnate Word has wished that His divine sign should be marked on our forehead. The forehead is the seat of modesty, and He wishes the Christian not to blush at the opprobrium of his Master. If, then, you make it in the presence of men, and are not ashamed of it, count on the divine mercy." [In Ps. 30. Enarr. iv. n. 8.]

The second, the honor of our forehead. "The Sign of the Cross," says Tertullian, "is the sign of foreheads, *signaculum frontium*." [Contr. Marcian, lib. v.]

And St. Augustine: "A forehead without the Sign of the Cross is a head without hair. The bald head is a subject of shame and derision. It is the same with the forehead unornamented with the Sign of the Cross. Such a forehead is impudent. Have you ever heard one Frenchman insulting another? He says to him; 'Vous n'avez pas de front (You have no forehead).' What does this mean? That he is impudent. May God preserve me from having a naked forehead; may the Cross of my Master ornament and cover it." [In Ps. 131.]

The third, the miracle of the Redemption. The Sign of the Cross is a trophy. Trophies are not placed in obscure corners, but in public places, where everybody can see them, and in seeing them be reminded of the triumphs of the conqueror. "Why then," cries out the great Augustine, "should not the

---

Trinity, was still much used in the thirteenth century. The second consists in extending five fingers, which recalls the five wounds of Our Lord. At present this is alone in use in the Church of the West.

Divine Word place on the forehead of man, on the most visible and noble of his members, the sign of victory won by the cross over the infernal powers?" [In Joan., Pract. xxxvi.]

By passing from places of execution to the brow of emperors, it was meet that the Cross should eternally proclaim the great miracle of the conversion of the world.

The fourth, the divine propriety. Re-entering into possession of man, the Divine Crucified has marked him with His seal, as the proprietor marks those things that belong to him.

"As soon as the Redeemer had restored man to his liberty," says St. Cæsarius of Arles, "He marked him with His sign. This sign is the cross. Engraved on the doors of palaces, we bear it on our forehead. It is the Conqueror who places it there, that all may know He has re-entered into possession of us, and that we are His palaces, His living temples. The demon also, jealous and furious, continually prowls around, seeking to rob us of the sign of our freedom, the charter of our liberty." [Homil. v. de pascha.]

The fifth, the dignity of man. The forehead is the noblest part of the body; it is, as it were, the seat of the soul. Whoever is master of the head is master of the man. Hence, of all parts of the human body, the forehead is that which the demon tries most furiously to deform. The deformation of this organ by artificial compression has been practiced all over the world; in many countries it still exists. To disfigure the image of God, to enfeeble the intellectual faculties, to develop the basest instincts; such are the established results of this deformation, humanly inexplicable. Our Lord, the Repairer of all things, wished that the Sign of Cross should, by preference, be marked on the forehead, in order to deliver it, and in delivering it, to restore to man, with the plenitude of his faculties, all the dignity of his being.

Respect is another condition required to make the Sign of the Cross well. Respect, because it is an act of religion, venerable for four reasons; for its origin, for its antiquity, for the use which has been made of it by the greatest and holiest men the world has ever seen, the apostles, martyrs and true Catholics of the primitive Church and of every age; and for the glory with which the Sign of the Cross shall shine on the last day, when, announcing the coming of the Sovereign Judge, it shall appear in the clouds, brilliant with light, and be placed with dignity beside the supreme tribunal, for the consolation of the just, and the eternal confusion of the wicked.

With attention; without this, the redeeming sign is no more than a mechanical movement, too often useless to ourselves, and perhaps injurious to Him, whose majesty, love and benefits it recalls.

With confidence; but a confidence filial, lively, strong, founded on the testimony of ages, on the practice of the Church, and the marvelous effects produced by this sign, formidable to the demon, and the liberator of man and the world.

With devotion; which places the heart in union with the lips. In making the Sign of the Cross what do I do? I proclaim myself the disciple, the brother, the friend, the child of a crucified God. Under pain of lying to myself and to God, I must be all that I say.

Listen to our forefathers. "When you sign yourself, think of all the mysteries contained in the Cross. It is not enough to form it simply with the finger; it is necessary first to make it with faith and good-will   .   .   .   When you mark your breast, your eyes, and all your members with the Sign of the Cross, offer yourself as a victim pleasing to God . . . If in marking yourself with the Sign of the Cross, you proclaim yourself a Christian soldier, yet, at the same time do not practice according to your ability, either charity, justice, or chastity, the Sign of the Cross avails you nothing. The Sign of the Cross is a great thing; it should be employed to mark only great and precious things. What use would it be to set a golden seal on hay or mud? What signifies the Sign of the Cross on the forehead and lips, if the soul be interiorly filled with crimes and stains?" [S. Chrys., Homil. 55, in Matth. S. Ephr., De adorat. vivif. cruc. S. Aug., Serm., 215, de Temp.—Signum maximum atque sublime. Lact., div. instit., lib. iv. c. 26.]

"To make the Sign of the Cross, and yet sin, what is this to be? It is to place the sign of life on the mouth, and to plunge the poniard into the heart." [S. Cæs., Serm. 278., inter Augustin.]

Hence the proverb of the primitive Christians: "*Habete Christurn in cordibus et signum ejus in frontibus*: (Brothers, have Jesus Christ in the heart, and His Sign on the forehead)." [Bed., t. 111, in collact. flor et parab.]

Hence, also, the saying of St. Augustine: "God asks not for painters, but for operators of His mysteries. If you bear on your forehead the sign of the humility of Jesus Christ, bear in your heart the imitation of the humility of Jesus Christ." [S. Aug., Ser. 32.]

We have every reason to act thus. Let no one say: "To make the Sign of the Cross, either well or ill, is of little importance." Christian ages have taught differently, so also has the Catholic Church, the Mistress of truth, so also has the Truth in person. Admitting even that the Sign of the Cross is of little importance, has not the Incarnate Word said: "He that is faithful in little things will be faithful in great; as he who is unfaithful in little things will be unfaithful in great?"

Is it not this daily fidelity which forms the Christian life and prepares the eternal recompense? In the affair of salvation, as in all other affairs, *that which suffices is not sufficient.* He who wishes to do only what is necessary, will not do even that for very long.

Ten times a day I make the Sign of the Cross. If it is well made, behold ten more good works, ten more degrees of glory and happiness for all eternity. Behold ten more pieces of money to pay my debts, or those of my brethren on earth or in purgatory, ten more instances to obtain the conversion of sinners and the perseverance of the just; to free the world and creatures from diseases, dangers and scourges. Compute the sum of merits accumulated at the end of a week, a year, a life-time of fifty years. And yet you say that this is of little importance!

You now know, dear Frederic, the Sign of the Cross, and the manner of making it. Let me confide to you an ambitious thought: Suppose a stranger arrives in Paris, and asks which is the young man, who, among all in this vast capital, makes the Sign of the Cross best. I wish that you might be named. At this price, I promise you a life worthy of our ancestors of the primitive Church, a death precious before God, and perhaps, the honors of canonization: *In hoc vince: By this sign thou shalt conquer.*

This divine saying is ever ancient, yet ever new, for it is the formula of a law. Constantine, who first deserved to hear it, is the type of man. The great emperor was advancing by forced marches to attack Maxentius, a dreadful tyrant who was in possession of the capital of the world. Suddenly, in calm weather, a little after midday, there appears in the heavens the

Sign of the Cross, brilliant with light, and visible to Constantine and the whole army, with the inscription: *By this sign thou shalt conquer: In hoc vince.*

The following night, the Son of God appears to the emperor, holding in His hand the same sign, and commands him to make one like it, to be carried in all his battles, and to be to him the pledge of victory.

Constantine obeys. The heavenly sign, resplendent with gold and precious stones, dazzles the eyes of his legions, and becomes the celebrated Labarum. Wherever this sacred ensign appears, confidence animates the soldiers of Constantine, terror seizes those of Maxentius. The Roman eagles fly before the cross, paganism before Christianity; satan, the ancient tyrant of Rome and the world, before Jesus Christ, the Saviour of Rome and the world. And thus it should be.

Maxentius being defeated and drowned, Constantine enters into Rome. A statue is erected, representing him holding the cross in his hand, with the following inscription directed by himself: "It is by this salutary sign, the true emblem of strength, that I have delivered your city from the yoke of tyranny, and that, giving liberty to the Senate and Roman people, I have re-established them in their ancient majesty and splendor." [Euseb., Vit Constant., lib. c. 33]

Constantine represents you, me, every baptized soul, the whole Christian world. Thrown into the arena of life, we march at the head of our senses and faculties, to attack a tyrant far more dangerous than Maxentius. Our Rome is heaven; he tries to prevent our entrance into it. He advances against us at the head of his infernal legions. The combat is inevitable. God gives us the same means of conquering that He gave to the son of Constantius; the Sign of the Cross; *In hoc vince.* Now, as formerly, this sign is the *formido dæmonum*, (terror of demons). Let us make it with faith, and the way to the eternal City shall be opened to us. Conquerors, and conquerors for ever, our gratitude will erect, in the sight of the angels and the elect, a statue bearing Constantine's inscription:

"It is by this sign, the true emblem of strength, that I have vanquished the demon, delivered my soul and body from his tyranny, and that, by giving to my senses, faculties, and entire being, their true liberty, I have established them for all eternity in the splendors of unlimited, unalloyed glory: *In hoc vince.*"

Hail, then, I will say, borrowing the language of the Fathers and Doctors of the East and the West—"Hail, Sign of the Cross, Standard of the great King, immortal trophy of the Lord, sign of life, sign of salvation, sign of benediction, terror of satan and the infernal legions, impregnable rampart, impenetrable buckler, invincible armor, royal sword, honor of the forehead, hope of Christians, remedy of the sick, resurrection of the dead, guide of the blind, support of the feeble, consolation of the poor, joy of the good, dread of the wicked, check to the rich, ruin of the proud, judge of the unjust, liberty of slaves, glory of martyrs, chastity of virgins, virtue of the saints, foundation of the Church!" [Gretzer, lib. iv. c. 64, etc]

You now have, dear Frederic, my answer to your two questions.

The authority of all ages resolves them in your favor. This triumphant apology for your noble conduct, will, I hope, arm you forever against mockeries and sophisms.

On one side, you know how important, and how solidly established is the habitual practice of the Sign of the Cross; and, on the other, you have the means of appreciating, at its just value, the intelligence of those who do not make it, as also of esteeming as it merits, the character of those who are ashamed to make it. *In hoc vince.*

Mgr. J.J. Gaume

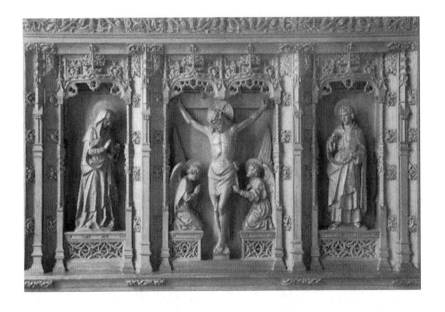

May this work be to all who read it, a fruitful source of the blessings promised herein.

THE TRANSLATOR.

IN HOC
SIGNO
VINCES!

Made in the USA
Lexington, KY
11 September 2017